MASSAGE

AND THE ORIGINAL SWEDISH MOVEMENTS

OSTROM

MASSAGE

AND THE ORIGINAL SWEDISH MOVEMENTS

LECTURES BEFORE THE TRAINING SCHOOLS FOR NURSES CONNECTED WITH THE HOSPITAL OF THE UNIVERSITY OF PENNSYLVANIA, GERMAN HOSPITAL, WOMAN'S HOSPITAL, PHILADELPHIA LYING-IN CHARITY HOSPITAL, THE PHILADELPHIA POLYCLINIC AND COLLEGE FOR GRADUATES IN MEDICINE, AND THE KENSINGTON HOSPITAL FOR WOMEN, OF PHILADELPHIA.

KURRE W. OSTROM

FROM THE
ROYAL UNIVERSITY OF UPSALA,
SWEDEN

INSTITUTE OF HEALTH SCIENCES

Distributed for the Institute of Health Sciences
by the Octagon Press Ltd

ISBN 0 9518025 0 X

First published in this edition 1991

Printed in Great Britain by
Redwood Press Limited, Melksham, Wiltshire

Introduction

When one of my students brought me a copy of this book, I read it with delight. Even the illustrations, it seemed to me, had a special charm. And Ostrom's text, the description of the massage movements and his advice to therapists are often as relevant today as they were nearly a century ago.

We have all heard the term *Swedish massage*, but – enquiring about it for two decades – I had been unable to locate a comprehensive account of what it was all about.

And here, at last, Pir Henrik Lings' original massage movements, which he used in conjunction with exercises, are charmingly brought to life.

When I first started practising massage, in the early 1960s, I was determined that something so fundamentally beneficial to us all – and used at all times and in all other human societies as an integral part of health care – should one day have a prominent and respected place in our society as well.

Why, I wondered, should Greece, Rome, India, China and Egypt – our precursors in civilisation – have the advantages of massage while it was denied to us?

Now, after thirty years, the dream has come true: massage is widely appreciated for the part it plays in maintaining health.

There has, it is true, been much to build upon; for massage had, in Ostrom's time already been a part of university and postgraduate training in Sweden, the United States and elsewhere. Indeed, this very book once fulfilled a teaching function in these institutions.

Few people remember that massage was formerly a legitimate subject taught in medical schools in Britain.

Now, massage as a complementary therapy in contemporary Britain has once again been officially accepted under appropriately distinguished auspices. We are teaching massage under the aegis of the Royal College of Nursing. The Clare Maxwell-Hudson School has held numerous medical postgraduate courses at teaching hospitals. We are proud to have played our part in restoring the practice to its rightful therapeutic place.

We are also, of course, grateful to the Heads of Departments who have supported our efforts so generously.

Medical knowledge has progressed so much since 1900 that this book should not now be used as a textbook. None of the advice given in it is valid without careful consideration of contemporary knowledge.

We have reprinted this text for its great charm and historical interest; but must stress that no medical condition is ever to be treated without medical supervision.

Since such professional supervision and collaboration is today increasingly and generously being given to us in the massage field by medical professionals, it seems all the more appropriate that this present piece of documentation be made available to an ever-widening audience.

Many thanks are due to Gill Frost for giving me a copy of this book. I hope that you enjoy it as much as she and I did.

Clare Maxwell-Hudson

PREFACE TO THE FIRST EDITION

As the tendency of modern therapeutics is to cure disease by the application of the laws of hygiene, the author feels that in presenting this little work to the medical profession, and to those especially interested in the subject, he will be supplying in English a treatise that has long been needed.

It is true, several books have been written on this subject by physicians, but none of them has been sufficiently explicit in telling how to perform the various manipulations, or the cases which may be benefited by the movements.

This work endeavors to explain how the movements are to be applied to all parts of the body, and also to show for what diseases such movements are indicated.

I am very much indebted to Drs. Charles K. Mills and H. Augustus Wilson for their kindness in giving me ample opportunity to practically demonstrate the Swedish methods of massage and movements at the Philadelphia Polyclinic and College for Graduates in Medicine.

I am also under obligations to several other professors of the same institution for valuable information received.

In describing the various movements and their influence upon the different parts of the body, I have consulted such well-known Swedish authors as *Wretlind*, *Hartelius*. *Kleen*, etc.

It is hoped that this little text-book will be a practical and valuable addition to what has already been published on the subject of mechanotherapy.

THE AUTHOR.

CONTENTS

MASSAGE

AND

THE SWEDISH MOVEMENTS

INTRODUCTION

Manual treatment for disease has to a certain extent existed since the creation. Man had, by instinct, acquired the art of manipulation long before nature yielded her secrets in medicine. This is still the practice among many nations. In Sweden, even at the present time, certain manipulations are used among the peasants for cramps, swellings, etc. The Swedes seem never to have lost the art—but recently revived in other countries.

Amiot and Dally speak of a perfect system of gymnastics among the Chinese three thousand years before the Christian era. They maintained that gymnastics, by preventing stagnation, produced an even and harmonious movement of the fluids in the human body, which is necessary to health. Not only did they use gymnastics to preserve health, but they also had a thorough knowledge of their therapeutic effects. From each of the natural positions they placed the body and limbs in certain derivative positions, which modified the movement of the fluids and were, of course, important in different diseases.

The priests of Egypt used some manipulation in the form of kneading and friction for rheumatic pains, neuralgias, and swellings.

The Hindoos, also, had some knowledge of their therapeutic importance; but the masses were soon mystified by the priests, who by incantations and magical words, led them to believe they were invented by the gods.

Even the Persians used a few movements for different affections.

The Greeks were the first to recognize gymnastics as an institution—a fact of much importance to the free states. Here they were auxiliary to the development of the people both socially and politically. The gymnasts were political, pedagogic, esthetic, and therapeutic. The philosophers and the physicians *recommended* manual treatment. Plato even divided it into active and passive movements, and especially recommended the latter. Some physicians practised the movements themselves; but there arose a class of people, called *Pädotribes*, some of whom acquired great skill in the manipulation of the human body.

Although the Romans imitated the Greeks to some extent, they rather preferred calisthenics; yet the manual method was more extensively practised in Rome under the emperors than it had hitherto been by any other nation.

Thus we see that among the ancients the most common movements were a few passive manipulations, while in the Middle Ages the gymnastics of an earlier period were more or less forgotten.

In the fifteenth and sixteenth centuries well-known physicians recommended gymnastics. Fuller and Tissot wished to combine the movements with the study of medicine. In the early part of the last century a therapeutic system of gymnastics acquired a reputation heretofore unknown, in movements based upon a certain action between operator and patient.

The Swede, P. H. Ling (1776-1839), and his predecessors, erected the first scientific system, in which they adopted the new medical science, making the movement treatment a perfectly scientific remedy, worthy of the confidence of every educated man.

In our own time, Dr. Mezger, of Wiesbaden, has demonstrated certain passive movements, and arranged them into a system that is now indorsed by every intelligent physician.

EXERCISE IN THERAPEUTICS

In walking or riding, or even in some of the ordinary occupations of life, it is true that a person takes a certain amount of exercise, but there is no *method* in such movements.

It is easy to determine how much is to be done and how long it may be continued, but it will be a very difficult matter to *estimate* the amount of vital force necessary to carry these exercises into execution.

For instance, in walking, the strength of the motion depends not only upon the time and speed used, but also upon the weight of the body, supported by the lower extremities. In many cases the strength and tone of the muscles of the leg are not in proportion to the weight of the body.

This condition is exemplified in most of the calisthenic exercises.

When a person is practising calisthenics, the strength of the exercise depends upon the constitution and upon the weight and the natural activity of the body, which are not necessarily in proportion to the individual's strength.

For instance in jumping; to a person weighing one hundred pounds the exercise may be only light and agreeable, whereas to another, weighing two hundred pounds, the weight of whose body is out of proportion to the muscular strength, the same exercise might prove positively injurious.

Not being able to *estimate* the vital force used in the common exercises practised under the head of calisthenics, or in the different sports or games, they should not be classified under the name of **Medical** or **Remedial Gymnastics.** In the latter case it is necessary to be able to *estimate* the amount of force required in every movement, and apply it according to the strength of each individual.

The difference between the **Movement Treatment** and the common exercise does not consist only in the quantitative estimate of the movements.

In the exhilarating exercise of riding the motion is *general*, acting upon the entire body, no part being excepted. On the other hand, in walking or dancing the muscles of the legs are used almost exclusively, those of the arms not being brought into action at all. The dancing-master has well-developed muscles in his legs, whereas, unless he resorts to some special exercise for his arms, their muscles will not be in proportion to those of the legs.

Persons of *sedentary* habits, especially dressmakers and clerks, who have but little exercise of any kind, are sure to have an ill-developed muscular system. Unless such persons take exercise systematically, they are liable to injure themselves severely. Persons who try to excel in any one kind of athletics run great risks of exceeding their strength.

Thus we see it is impossible to *estimate* the benefit of calisthenics, which can easily be done with the Swedish movements.

Finally, in the **movement treatment,** all movements are arranged in such a way and in such a form as to be comfortable and adapted to all parts of the body.

Based upon a knowledge of the *anatomy* and *physiology* of the parts, and of their proper physiologic limits, this treatment is much superior to any other, as well as more agreeable.

All joints have a natural motion within certain fixed limits. When such joints are gently exercised, an agreeable sensation is produced; but if the exercise be too violent,—flexing, extending, or rotating to excess,—severe pains will probably result. The same may be said of the muscular system. Each muscle having a distinct and certain function to perform, proper exercise of these muscles, if confined to physiologic limits, will be invigorating and agreeable to the patient.

In giving the **Swedish movements** special attention is directed to the natural functions of joints and muscles. This is not the case with any other kind of exercise, consequently the sensation and value of promiscuous movements can never be the same.

When movements are necessary over painful parts of the body, the patient must sometimes judge how much he can bear.

An operator who is not able to explain the physiologic action of every manipulation or movement he uses is liable to do more harm than good to the patients.

The Swedish movement treatment can better adapt itself to all conditions than any other treatment.

Finally, the aim of the Swedish treatment is, by a careful manipulation of muscles and joints, to restore to good health such as are in any way diseased. The force of such manipulations can be estimated and the extent of their duration fixed.

MASSAGE

The word **Massage** is a derivation from the Greek *massein*, or the French *masser*, which both mean: *to knead*. A male operator is called a *masseur*, a female operator, a *masseuse*.

Massage *is a scientific treatment, by certain passive systematic manipulations, upon the nude skin of the human body.*

Dr. Mezger, of Amsterdam (now practising in Wiesbaden, Germany), and his two pupils, the Swedish physicians Berghman and Helleday, were among the first to apply the massage treatment scientifically. Their method is now used throughout Europe. According to Mezger, massage is a scientific treatment—*i.e.*, based upon the anatomy and the physiology of the human body; his manipulations are certain—that is, given or fixed, so that an uninstructed person can not pick up the treatment—it is an art that can not be self-acquired; all manipulations are passive—*i.e.*, applied to the patient without his assistance or resistance; the manipulations are also systematic—*i.e.*, they are arranged so as to act systematically upon the different tissues of the human body.

Dr. Mezger divides the massage treatment into four principal manipulations:

1. EFFLEURAGE.
2. FRICTIONS.
3. PÉTRISSAGE.
4. TAPOTEMENT.

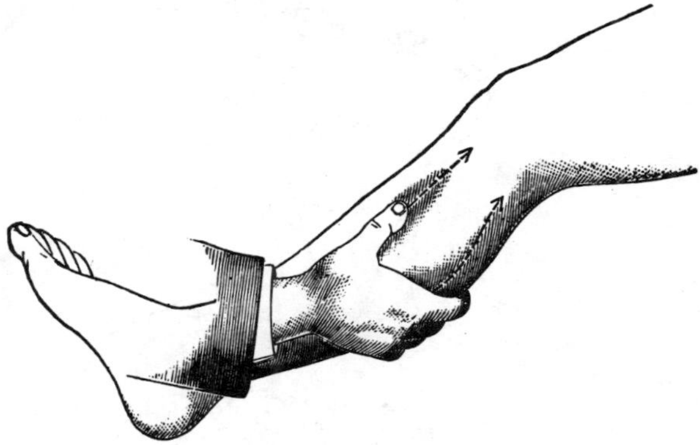

FIG. 1.—Stroking with One Hand.

1. EFFLEURAGE (STROKING)

This manipulation consists of centripetal (toward the body or heart) **Strokings.**

It is performed in four different ways:

(*a*) Stroking with the palm of one hand.

(*a*) Stroking with the palms of both hands.

(*c*) Stroking with the thumb.

(*d*) Stroking with the tips of the fingers.

STROKING WITH THE ONE HAND (see Fig. 1) is used upon the extremities, the back of the head, and in single massage of the neck (Gerst's method).

Stroking with Both Hands is used upon the lower extremities of adults, upon the chest (see Fig. 2) and back, also in double massage of the neck.

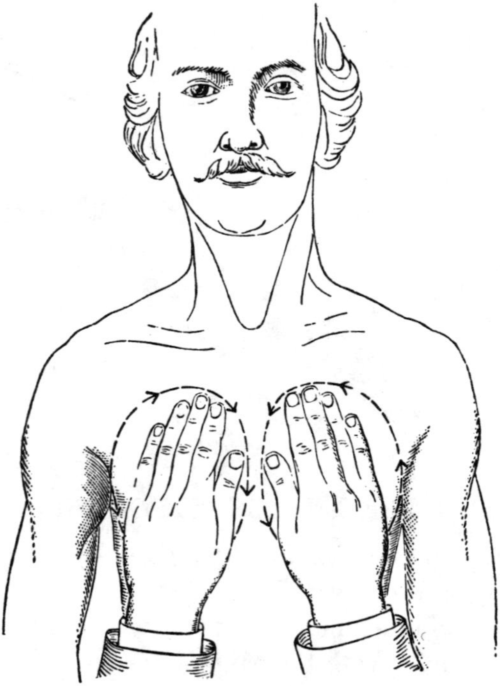

Fig. 2.—Stroking with Both Hands.

Stroking with the Thumb (see Fig. 3) is used between two muscles, or between a muscle and a tendon; also frequently to reach the *interossei* in the hands and the feet.

STROKING WITH THE TIPS OF THE FINGERS (see Fig. 4), or the last two phalanges, is principally

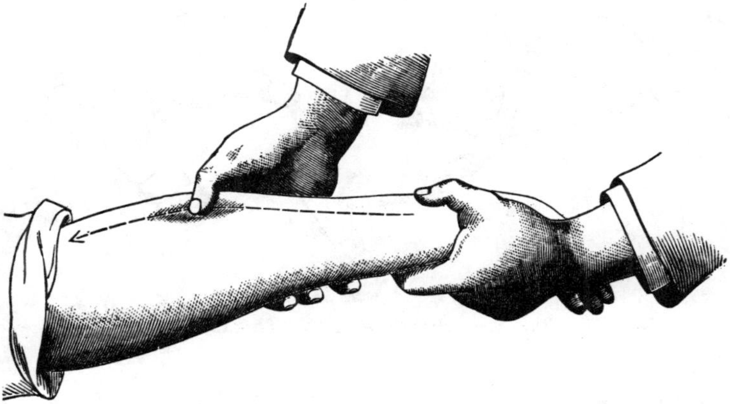

FIG. 3.—Stroking with the Thumb.

used around the joints (in cases of sprains, etc.), the fingers conforming themselves to the shape of the part to be worked upon.

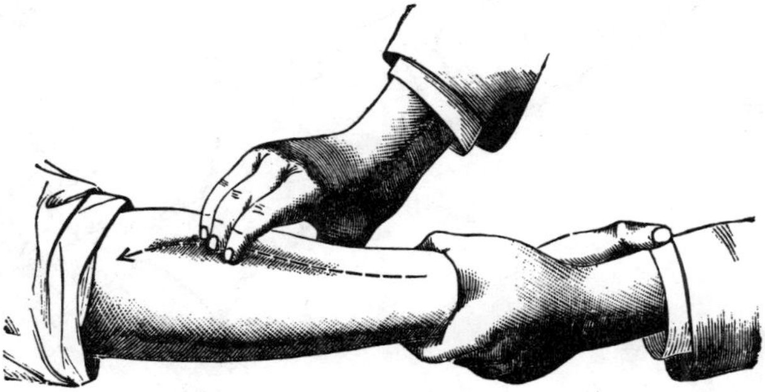

FIG. 4.—Stroking with the Tips of the Fingers.

The strength of the manipulation, stroking, varies from the slightest touch to the strongest

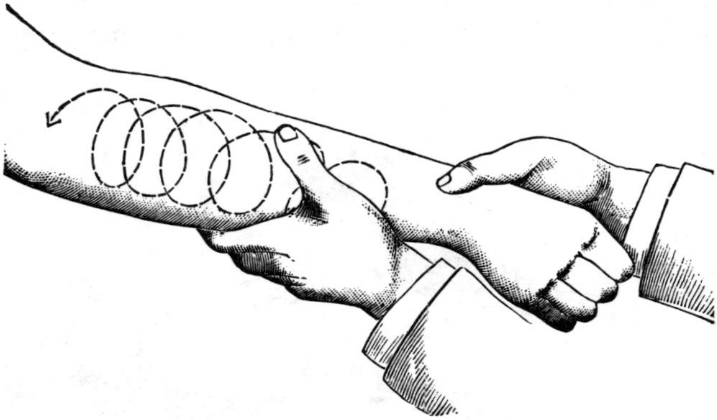

FIG. 5.—Friction with the Thumb.

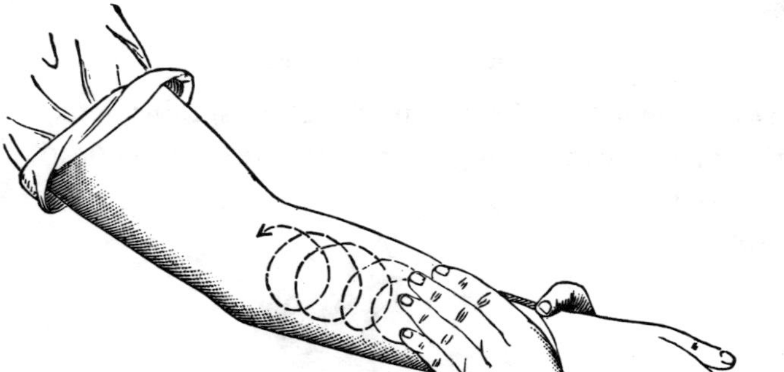

FIG. 6.—Friction with the Tips of the Fingers.

pressure; even with one hand on top of the other, if necessary.

The aim of all STROKINGS *is to increase the circulation in the venous blood-vessels and the lymphatics, thereby causing absorption.*

FIG. 7.—Kneading with the Two Thumbs.

2. FRICTIONS (FRICTION)

Are firm, circular manipulations, always followed by centripetal strokings. As a rule, they are performed over one group of muscles at a time.

Friction is given in three different ways:

(*a*) Friction with the thumb.

(*b*) Friction with the tips of the fingers.

(*c*) Friction with the one hand.

Friction with the Thumb (see Fig. 5) is used upon the extremities, but also upon smaller surfaces; as, for instance, around the knee-joints and upon the facial muscles (see Fig. 113).

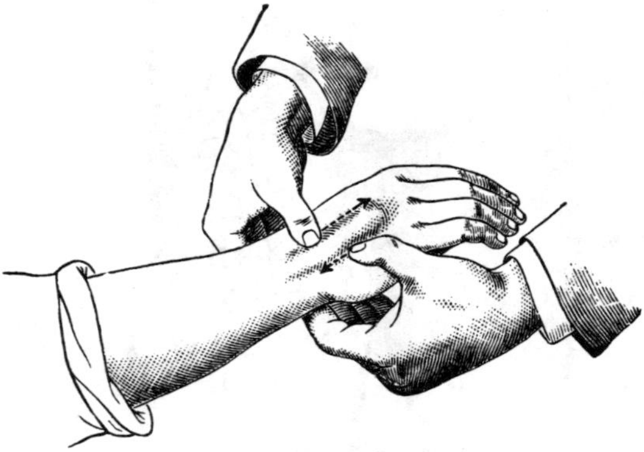

Fig. 8.—Kneading on the Hand, for Contracted Tendons and Muscles.

Friction with the Tips of the Fingers is used around the joints, the thumb often supporting the hand (see Fig. 6). The circles are sometimes made a great deal smaller than demonstrated in Fig. 6.

Friction with the One Hand is used upon the larger surfaces and fleshier parts, like the thigh, arm proper, and lumbar region of back.

All FRICTIONS should be centripetal, and should *always* be followed by centripetal strokings, *as the aim of this manipulation is to transform pathologically changed parts into a condition that will*

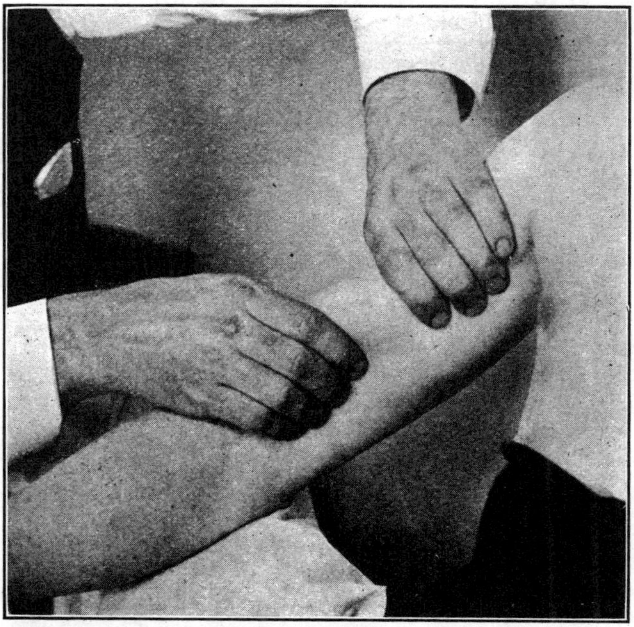

FIG. 9.—Kneading (Pétrissage) of Biceps.

permit them to be incorporated into the healthy tissues, and thence be absorbed by the veins and lymphatics.

3. PÉTRISSAGE (KNEADING)

This manipulation is performed in such a manner as to cause a double centripetal pressure on a tissue (muscle or tendon), at the same time raising it up from its normal point of attachment.

We have three different kinds of **Pétrissage:**

(*a*) Kneading with the two thumbs.

(*b*) Kneading with the thumb and fingers.

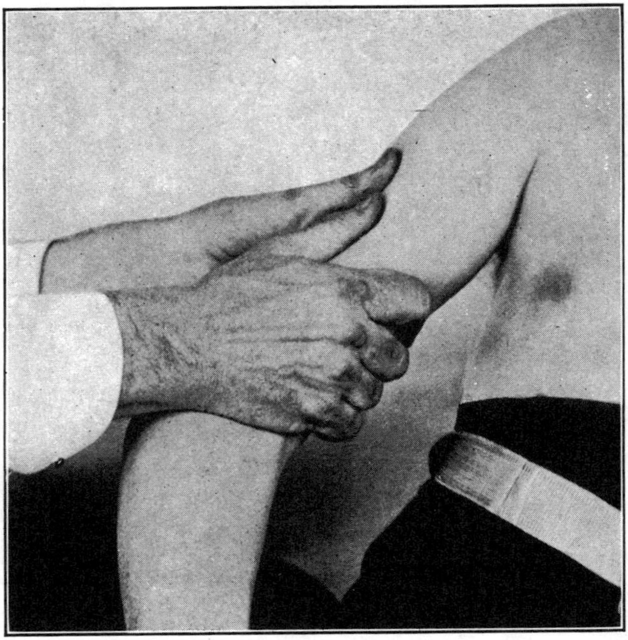

FIG. 10.—Kneading with Both Hands.

(*c*) Kneading with the two hands.

KNEADING WITH THE TWO THUMBS (see Figs. 7 and 8) is used to reach individual muscles.

KNEADING WITH THE THUMB AND FINGERS, which manipulation is called PINCHING (see Fig.

9), is also used to reach individual muscles, but is preferred on a deep-seated tissue.

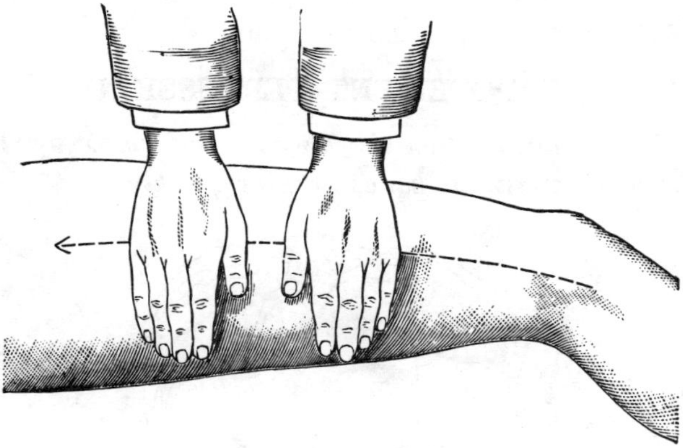

FIG. 11.—Clapping of the Leg.

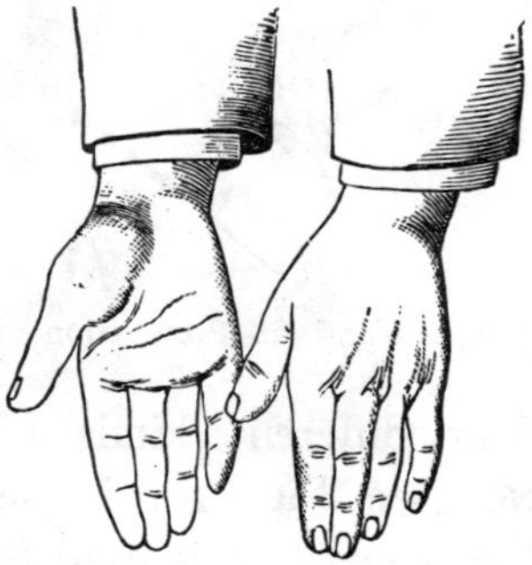

FIG. 12.—Position of Hands in Hacking.

KNEADING WITH BOTH HANDS, called SQUEEZING, is used upon the lower extremities, and upon the arm proper (see Fig. 10) of adults.

The aim of the manipulation KNEADING *is to reach the separate muscles with a firm double pressure and expose them to an action similar to that of* FRICTION.

4. TAPOTEMENT (PERCUSSION)

This manipulation is always performed by the operator's wrist, the hands striking quickly.

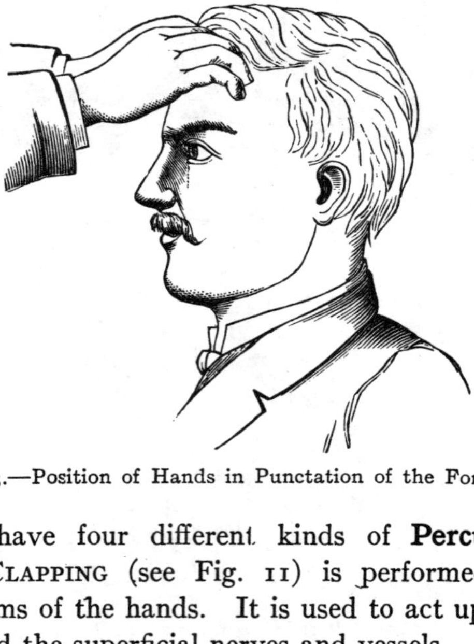

FIG. 13.—Position of Hands in Punctation of the Forehead.

We have four different kinds of **Percussion:**

(*a*) CLAPPING (see Fig. 11) is performed with the palms of the hands. It is used to act upon the skin and the superficial nerves and vessels.

In clapping it is advisable to spread a towel over the skin to avoid stinging.—(*Editor*).

(*b*) HACKING (see Fig. 12) is performed with

the ulnar border of the hand. It is used around nerve centers and upon the muscles.

(*c*) PUNCTATION (see Fig. 13) is performed with the tips of the fingers. It is used upon the head and in circles around the heart.

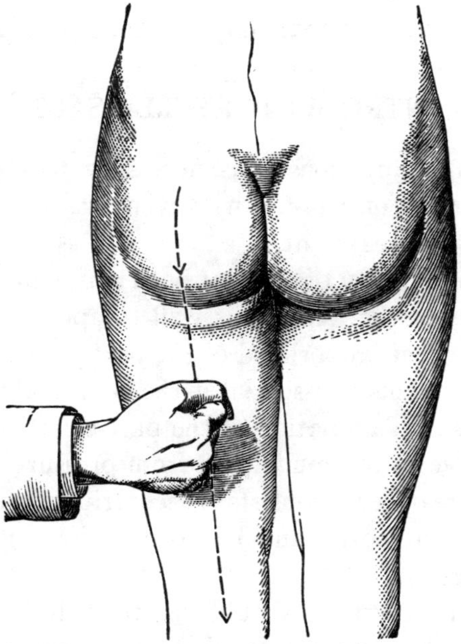

FIG. 14.—Beating over the Sciatic Nerve.

(*d*) BEATING (see Fig. 14) is performed by the clenched hand. It is used upon the glutei and upon the lower extremities over the *sciatic* nerve.

MASSAGE AS A THERAPEUTIC AGENT

is divided into **Introductory, General** and **Local.**

INTRODUCTORY MASSAGE

In many affections it is necessary to commence the operation of massage with what has been termed *introductory* treatment.

In the majority of cases of both acute and chronic affections of the joints it is well to apply the treatment to the neighborhood of the part, and especially above it. This is essential if the skin is abraded or if a severe inflammation of the part exists rendering it sensitive to too much pain from pressure.

The treatment consists of centripetal strokings (with one or both hands) in connection with a few kneadings.

Special attention should be paid to the inside parts of the extremities where the principal veins and lymphatics pass. If possible and convenient, always try to get the aid of gravity by elevation.

By this treatment we prepare the venous and lymphatic systems to absorb the diseased particles subsequently expelled from the affected part.

If for instance we have a case of synovitis of the

knee-joint we commence by stroking the inside part of the thigh, slightly elevating the lower part of the extremity so as to get the aid of gravity. The introductory massage in treating circulatory and nervous affections of the head consists of Hoeffinger's method of massage of the neck so as to procure a free outlet for the venous blood from the head.

In the treatment of hemorrhoids by massage we should always commence by treating the liver, thereby procuring an outlet for the congested blood of the abdomen through the portal vein. When taken in time massage is really a specific in the treatment of hemorrhoids.

This is mentioned only to emphasize the importance of the introductory massage in all manual treatment. The success of massage used in joint affections will often depend upon how well and how judiciously the introductory treatment is applied.

GENERAL MASSAGE

By general massage we mean the treatment applied to the whole body, with the exception of the head.

The operator begins with the foot, stroking with one hand or kneading with the thumbs. Then he proceeds with the legs, the arms, the chest, the abdomen, and finally the back. All the manipulations may be used, and special attention should be given to the hacking. Some authors advise to first take the extremities, then the back, and finally the neck and abdomen (Kleen and others). With this treatment we generally combine a few passive rotations or flexions, similar to those recommended for anemia. The patient must be lying in bed, well covered on those parts not operated upon. It is of advantage for the operator to begin with the left foot and leg, and then have the patient turn over to the other side of the bed, where the balance of the treatment may be convenientl performed.

In regard to the time necessary to spend in giving general massage, I would advise the operator to begin with thirty minutes, and gradually increase the time so that one hour is consumed at the end of the first week. The length and the severity of the treatment should always be regulated by the patient's condition. General massage should not be employed until two hours have elapsed after meals. As soon as a part is operated upon it should be covered up at once.

LOCAL MASSAGE

By *local* massage we mean the treatment applied to the different parts of the body at one time; for instance, massage of the shoulder.

I. MASSAGE OF THE LEG

Position.—The patient is lying or half lying on a bed or couch. The operator sitting at his side performs the following manipulations:

1. Stroking of the foot sole and dorsum; quick stroking with the palm of the hand to the sole of the foot finishing with firm and quick clappings with one hand, the other grasping the ankle underneath, so as to elevate the limb.

2. Stroking with both hands from the ankle to the hip, the hand on the outside reaching up to the crest of the ilium, the thumb of the hand on the inside, with moderate pressure, going down toward the groin. (Avoid pressure upon the tibia.)

3. Friction with the thumb upon the outside of the leg from ankle to knee-joint, covering principally the flexors of the foot.

4. Stroking with one hand of the same part.

5. Friction with the thumb upon the inside and posterior part of the leg, covering principally the *gastrocnemius* and the *soleus*.

6. Stroking with one hand of the same part.

7. Friction with the thumb or hand upon the outside, inside and the back part of the thigh, dividing it into four distinct parts so as to thoroughly work upon all the different muscles.

8. Repeated strokings over the whole extremity, from ankle to hip.

9. Kneading with the two thumbs or both hands upon the different muscles of the whole extremity.

10. Hacking or clapping upon the whole extremity, avoiding the bones.

In certain cases (dropsy, rheumatism, etc.),

it is well to have the limb elevated, thereby promoting the return of the venous blood.

The limb should be frequently turned, so that the posterior part may receive proper attention.

II. MASSAGE OF THE ARM

Position.—The patient is sitting or lying, with the semiflexed arm supported, if convenient. The operator sits at the side.

1. Stroking with one hand on the outside of the arm, from the wrist to the trapezius. The other hand should support around the wrist, but care should be taken that no pressure be used over the radial artery, as that checks circulation considerably.

2. Stroking with the other hand upon the inside of the arm, from wrist to shoulder-joint, the thumb going out toward the pectoral muscles. Support is given in a similar manner as described in 1.

3. Friction with the thumb upon the extensors of the hand and fingers with repeated strokings of the same part.

4. Friction with the thumb of the other hand upon the flexors of the hand and fingers, with repeated strokings upon the same part.

5. Friction with the hand upon the arm proper.

6. Stroking of the whole arm, as described in 1 and 2.

7. Kneading with the two thumbs of both hands upon different muscles, special attention being paid

to reach the extensors and flexors in the forearm, the *biceps*, *triceps*, *deltoid*, *supraspinatus* and *infraspinatus*.

8. Hacking over the whole arm.

The most common mistakes in treating the arm are:

1. Too tight grasp around the wrist with the supporting hand.

2. The arm is kept too rigid, preventing the proper and necessary relaxation of the muscles.

3. The muscles of the upper part of the arm and shoulder are too often neglected.

4. Inefficient kneading.

III. MASSAGE OF THE CHEST

Position.—The patient is lying flat on the back, without head-rest, and the arms placed at the sides.

1. Stroking with both hands, one on each side of the sternum. The manipulation should be performed upward and inward, making a somewhat circular motion (see Fig. 2).

2. Friction with thumb over pectorales major and minor, with repeated strokings. Always from the origin (sternum) toward the insertion (the arm).

3. Kneading with the thumb and fingers (pinching) if the muscles of the one side be paralyzed.

4. Hacking or clapping over the chest may also be used, according to circumstances. Punctation in circles around the heart has also been recommended, but if used, great care should be taken.

As a rule, all percussions applied to the thorax should be used with discretion.

In massage of the breast place the hands at the outer circumference and by alternate frictions proceed upward to the nipple. In cases of caked breasts it is often necessary to use frictions with the tips of the fingers over hard places to relieve distended ducts. Always finish the treatment with the so-called "fulling" consisting of gentle pressure from the base of the breast upward with both hands alternately. Massage with camphorated oil is a great relief in over-distended breasts. The operator should always be careful not to bruise the glands in any way, as tumors are liable to develop in after years and cause no end of trouble. Massage and exercise are the only means by which the bust can be properly developed. The patient should be taught how to breathe properly and for the quick development of the mammary glands use in the massage as above described the following preparation, recommended by Dr. W. J. Haynes:

Lanoline	2 ounces
Cocoa Butter	2 ounces
Oil Cajeput	1 ounce
Oil Sassafras	½ ounce
Extract Saw Palmetto	2 ounces

This preparation has not a fine odor, but produces a pleasant sensation in the skin. It is a valuable compound wherever we wish to develop a part, but should not be used on the face.

IV. MASSAGE OF THE BACK

Position.—The patient is lying on his face, without the head-rest; the arms should be kept at the sides.

1. Stroking with both hands, one on each side of the spinal column, from the base of the skull

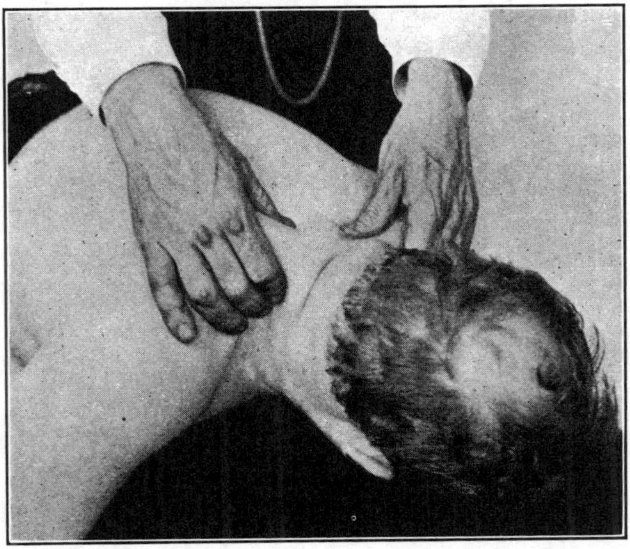

FIG. 15.—Pinching on the Sides so as to act on Sympathetic Ganglia.

down to the sacrum. If on a large person, the operator had better divide the back into three parts, in such a manner as to first work next to the spinal column, then over the center of the back, and finally over the sides, remembering that by the last manipulation he may conveniently reach the liver or spleen, if desirable in certain cases. In the case of an infant, and especially in infantile paralysis, we often use in the stroking only the index and the middle fingers, one on each side of the spinal column.

2. Friction with the hand or with the last two phalanges of the one hand, from the upper part of the trapezius down to the glutei, one side at a time.

3. Stroking as previously described.

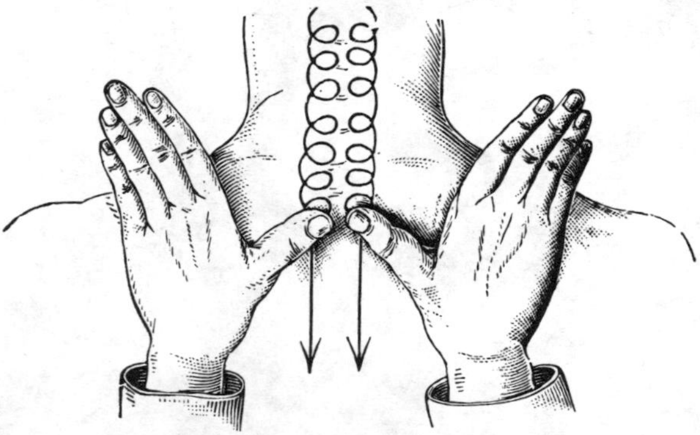

FIG. 16.—Kneading of the Back.

4. Kneading with the two thumbs, one on each side of the spine, so as to act upon the spinal nerves. The hands should be spread over the back, supporting the sides if possible (see Fig. 16).

5. Pinching on the sides so as to act upon the sympathetic ganglia (see Fig 15).

6. Hacking with one hand on each side of the spine, up and down, from the sacrum to the neck.

7. Clapping on both sides, lengthwise, one at a time (see Fig 17).

8. Stroking repeated; performed very quickly if we wish to stimulate; very slowly and firmly if we wish the manipulation to have a soothing effect.

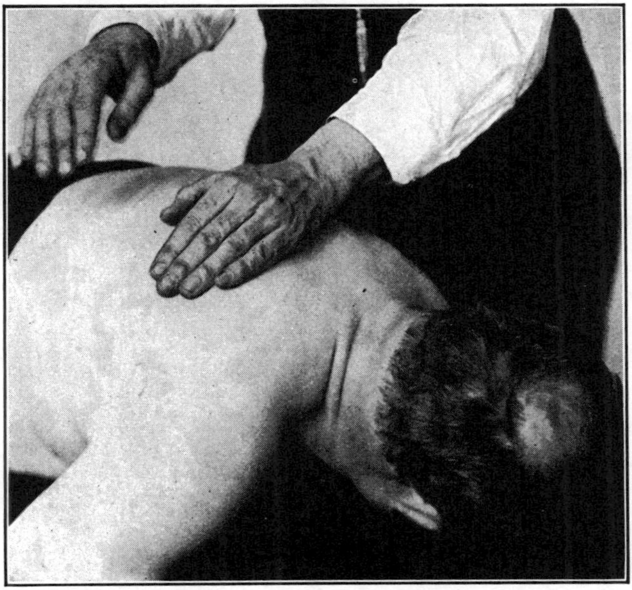

FIG. 17.—Clapping on Both Sides.

V. MASSAGE OF THE GLUTEI

Position.—The patient is standing with the body bent forward and supported on a lounge or bedstead. The operator stands behind and performs:

1. Stroking with both hands from the spine outward, downward (see Fig. 18).

2. Friction with the hand; one side at a time.

3. Beating in circles, one side at a time.

If the patient is suffering severe pain from standing the manipulation may be performed while he is

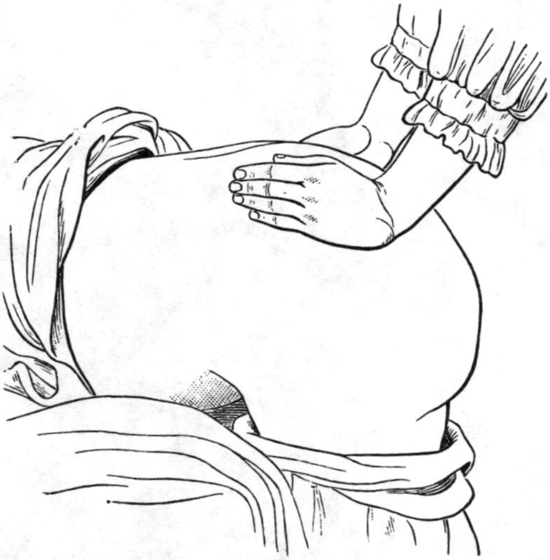

FIG. 18.—Stroking of the Glutei.

in bed, with a couple of pillows placed underneath his abdomen and thighs.

VI. MASSAGE OF THE ABDOMEN

Position.—The patient is lying flat on his back, generally without head-rest, and with the knees drawn up, so as to relax the abdominal muscles (see

Fig. 19). It is most convenient for the operator to sit at the patient's right side.

1. Friction with the tips of the fingers in circles *from right to left* over the umbilical region of the abdomen, thereby acting upon the *smaller intestine.* Begin with a very gentle pressure, gradually increasing the strength of the manipulation (see Fig. 20).

2. Spread the right hand over the abdomen so that the ball of the hand covers part of the *ascending colon;* press over that part upward to the *transverse*

FIG. 19.—Position in Massage of the Abdomen and the Ventricle.

colon; then stroke with the radial border of the hand firmly over to the left side. Here the tips of the fingers should be used for the downward pressure over the *descending colon.* The manipulation is repeated in circles without interruption (see Fig. 21).

These two manipulations are schematically illustrated in Figs. 20 and 21, and the operator should teach the patient how to perform them on himself every morning, particularly in cases of constipation.

A cannon ball covered with leather is also very

useful in manipulation No. 2, when the patient for some reason is obliged to do it himself. They can be procured from Charles Lentz and Sons, Philadelphia.

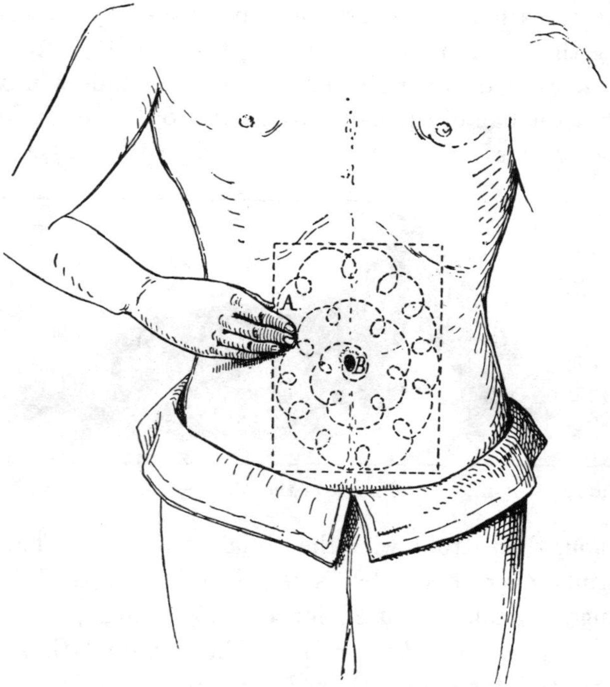

FIG. 20.

3. Kneading with the heel of the hand over the whole abdomen, going carefully at first and avoiding any sore places. Fecal lumps are often found and they should be gently and gradually broken up.

Near the sigmoid flexure we can sometimes accomplish more by substituting this manipulation for that of the friction with the tips of the fingers. The reason for that is that we can reach in deeper and

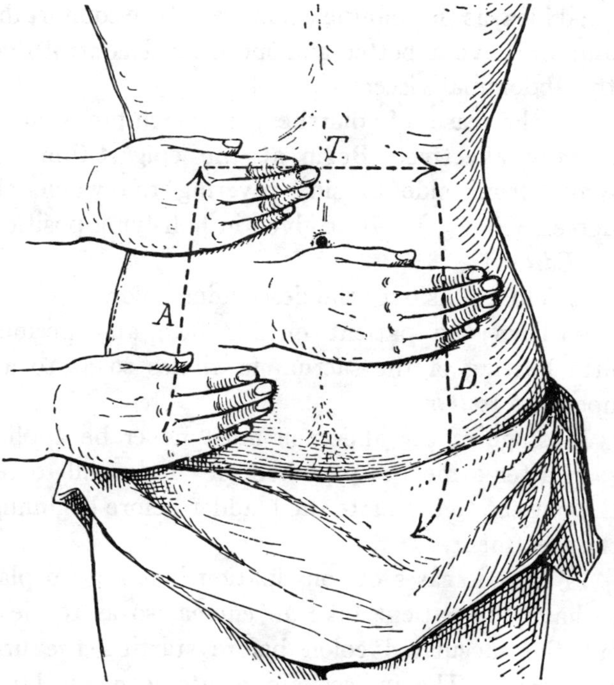

FIG. 21.

our efforts become more localized. The same refers to the breaking up of adhesions around the appendix and the ovaries.

This manipulation will sometimes produce an

unpleasant sensation at first, which is frequently caused by the patient not breathing properly. Talk to him so as to make him forget that he is being treated. Some operators place one hand as a support under the patient's back, and it is a very good idea, as the manipulation feels more comfortable and we have a better and more fixed control over the abdominal viscera.

In the case of diarrhea, stomach-pit shaking is very effective. Begin at the epigastrium and shake from side to side covering the whole abdomen (Fig. 34). Best given in half-lying position. —(*Editor*.)

4. Vibrations over the descending colon.

5. Turn the patient on his face and perform firm beating of the sacrum in circles so as to act upon the *rectum*.

Massage of the abdomen must never be applied soon after a meal is partaken of. It is well to tell the patient to evacuate the bladder before beginning the treatment.

In chronic cases of constipation it is a good plan to have the patient take an enema, so as to clean out the sacculated colon before starting the first treatment. The indiscriminate and continued use of injections will produce a relaxed condition of the bowel, while on the contrary massage will strengthen and stimulate to normal activity its various membranes.

VII. MASSAGE OF THE LIVER

Position.—The patient is lying half way turned over on his left side. The operator sits at his right side.

1. Friction with the palm of the hand in large circles covering gradually the entire organ.

2. Kneading with the heel of the hand.

3. Clapping over the entire organ, firmly over the right hypochondriac region, more gently over the epigastrium and left hypochondrium.

4. Palmar vibration over the different lobes.

5. Digital vibration, working the separated and bent fingers gradually under the curve of the ribs and costal cartilages.

Deep respiratory exercises are very important in connection with massage of the liver.

VIII. MASSAGE OF THE SPLEEN

Position.—The patient should, of course, lie on his right side. This treatment is performed in a similar way as massage of the liver.

IX. MASSAGE OF THE STOMACH

Several methods have been proposed to reach the ventricle by massage. They are all more or less dangerous, and we mention one of them only, for the completeness of the system.

Position.—The patient is lying flat on his back, as described on page 31, Fig. 19.

1. The operator sits at his side, and quietly placing his right hand, with abducted thumb, about two inches below the ribs of the left side, he performs strokings and frictions of the organ, from left to right. In dilatation of stomach use same grip, pressing upward under strong vibration. —(*Editor.*) Friction with the tips of the fingers is the most convenient form to use.

FIG. 22.—Stroking of the Forehead.

2. Kneading with the two thumbs may also be used, but the operator should always remember that he has to deal with very sensitive parts, consequently his pressure should be moderate.

3. Vibration with the tips of the fingers.

X. MASSAGE OF THE HEAD

Position.—The patient is sitting, comfortably supported.

1. Stroking.—Beginning with the back of the head, keeping the left hand firmly on the forehead, and with the right in a V-shape, stroke downward. In stroking the forehead place the thumbs between the eyebrows and stroke firmly over the temples to the ears, both thumbs working together, so as to act upon the supraorbital nerve (see Fig. 22).

2. Friction with the one hand, the other supporting, on the diagonally opposite part of the head. I have always found it best and most expedient to divide the head into four divisions for applying this manipulation, always beginning with the back part of the right side.

3. Friction with the tips of the fingers pressing firmly so as to move the scalp and to prevent breaking off the brittle or weakened hairs. This manipulation is particularly valuable when we work in a hair tonic. By working the scalp we draw the blood to the hair-roots (see Fig 23).

4. Hacking is used with both hands striking together, making circles over the head, beginning on the top and moving backward, downward, and forward to the starting point.

For increasing the hair growth the author has never found anything to equal the following treatment. Shampoo the head freely with a good, pure tar soap and let the lather remain for two hours, then wash it off with warm water, adding a little of some good tonic. Now massage the scalp thoroughly with crude petroleum and allow that to stay on over night. Of course the patient must wear a night-cap or in some other way protect the pillow-slip.

The author has experimented lately with the new oxygenated petroleum product, "Petrogen" (Wyeth),

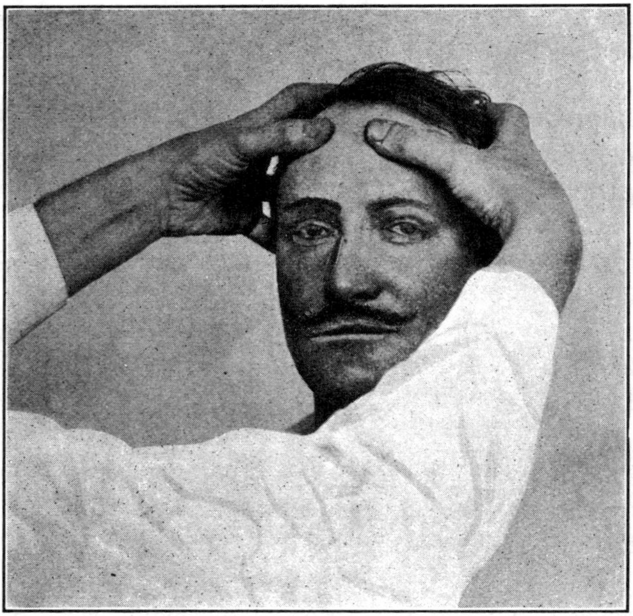

FIG. 23.—Friction with Tips of the Fingers.

as a base for a hair tonic and the results have been so exceptionally good that he begs to call the reader's special attention to it.

XI. MASSAGE OF THE FACE

Position.—The patient is lying or sitting with the head comfortably supported. Tell him to relax the muscles of the head and neck.

1. Stroking with the two thumbs over the forehead, starting near by the eyebrows gradually in succession working up to the hair-roots as in Fig. 22.

2. Friction with the tips of the fingers in small circles, the other hand being used to stretch the part worked upon; for this manipulation divide the forehead in two sections vertically. This is principally applied with the object of overcoming wrinkles of the forehead.

3. Repeated stroking as in No. 1, the operator being careful to tightly grasp the temples, so as to make the patient feel that the head is properly supported.

4. Stroking with the tips of the fingers over and below the eyes from the nose outward to the temples, both sides at a time.

5. Friction with the tips of the fingers over the same part with special attention to the outer corner of the eye and below it, where we generally find the so-called "*crow feet.*" Stretch the part with the thumb and fingers of one hand, and perform the friction with the tips of the fingers of the other hand.

6. Repeated strokings as in No. 4.

7. Stroking with the two index-fingers over the nose from the eyebrows downward and outward.

Raise the hands up high and hold them so during the manipulation from start to finish. In other words, the heel of the hand should be on a level with the tip of the finger.

8. Stroking with both hands one on each side of the face from the extreme lower part of the inferior maxillary region well up to the temple. We stroke upward because the face frequently presents a drawn and pulled-down appearance; particularly so after a prolonged illness or a siege of nervous worry or tension.

9. Friction and kneading of the cheeks, picking up the muscles as much as possible, always remembering that the orbicularis oris is the insertion of most all the principal facial muscles.

10. Repeated strokings as in No. 8, only the patient is told to inflate his cheeks and to retain the air, breathing freely through his nose.

11. Stroking with the fingers around the lips and chin.

12. Frictions with the tips of the fingers over the same part of kneading if our object is to remove superfluous fat. In the latter case never use any fatty ointment, but instead some benzoin preparation that will help to contract the tissues.

13. Strokings repeated, as described in No. 11.

In treating wrinkles the operator should remember that they are not, as a rule, caused by some trouble in the skin itself, but mostly always by a relaxed or weakened condition of the underlying muscular tissues; consequently our work must not be superficial but deep, care being taken, of course, not to bruise the patient. By stimulating the circulation to this particular part, we bring in increased nourishment to the relaxed and weakened tissues. It is really wonderful what can be done in the way of improving the facial expression by scientific massage, but like other parts of this valuable therapeutic, it has been horribly abused. Steaming the face is frequently practised but it is not to be recommended inasmuch as it frequently causes the patient to contract a severe cold. Facial paralysis and "tic douloureux" have been traced to steaming of the face. A massage operator who can not, by his manipulations, bring enough blood to the relaxed parts should not treat a face! Scars are treated by stretching the part and working with the tips of the fingers in circles across the scar-tissue, finishing with strokings. Never use an ointment for facial massage that contains vaselin or lanolin. They are both apt to produce hair growth, particularly the former. There are so many inferior preparations on the market, that the author feels prompted to here give a recipe for a very good facial skin food known, and in the many years he has recommended it, he has never heard anything but the very best results from it.

Oil of Sweet Almonds	2 ounces
Spermaceti	¼ ounce
White Wax	¼ ounce
Orange fl. water	½ ounce

It will be noticed that there are no mineral fats amongst the ingredients. Care should be taken to see that the genuine spermaceti and wax be used, as both these preparations are "made" from coal oil and we should not be willing to risk

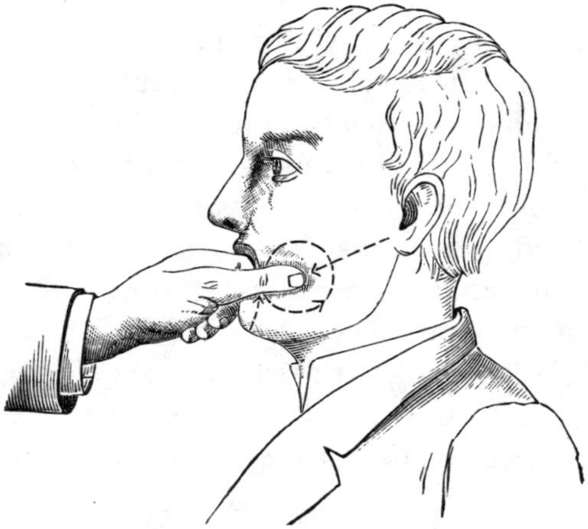

FIG. 24.—Massage of the Face.

causing a hair growth on the face. If we wish to make the eyebrows thicker and wider we can do so with the aid of coal oil preparations, but it must be done by a trained person. Mr. C. Keeny, 1601 Arch Street, Philadelphia, prepares the above-mentioned "Skin-food" and it can be obtained from him at any time.

In cases of facial paralysis it becomes necessary to work somewhat differently than previously described. Cover the antiseptically cleaned index-finger with a rubber tip or a silk handkerchief, insert it in the mouth and with the thumb stroke the muscles in the superior and inferior maxillary regions (see Fig. 24). The index acts as a good and easily regulated support. Friction and kneading are given in a similar way. In applying vibrations to the facial nerves and muscles, the author has used with the greatest satisfaction the mechanical vibrator made by the Vibratile Company of New York City.

There are now many different vibrators on the market and the masseur should have at least one of them. Most of them are run by power obtained from the electric street current. Unfortunately this form of massage has been taken up by the barbers, many of whom use it without thought and discretion.

XII. MASSAGE OF THE EYE

Position.—The patient sits with the head leaning backward, the operator standing at his side.

1. The index-finger is placed on his eyebrow, the middle finger grasping the eyelid, which is pressed, with either a radial or circular motion, against the eye. Be very careful not to use too much strength, and perform the movement as quickly as possible (see Fig. 25).

By placing the index on the eyebrow we take the weight of the heavy hand off the tender organ. The lid really performs the massage by pressure generated through the finger.

2. Vibrations with the fingers (see Fig. 37). While it is understood that the operator's hands should at all times be scrupulously clean, it becomes necessary to always use a mild antiseptic before treating the eyes.

XIII. MASSAGE OF THE THROAT

Position.—The patient is sitting, in a somewhat reclining position.

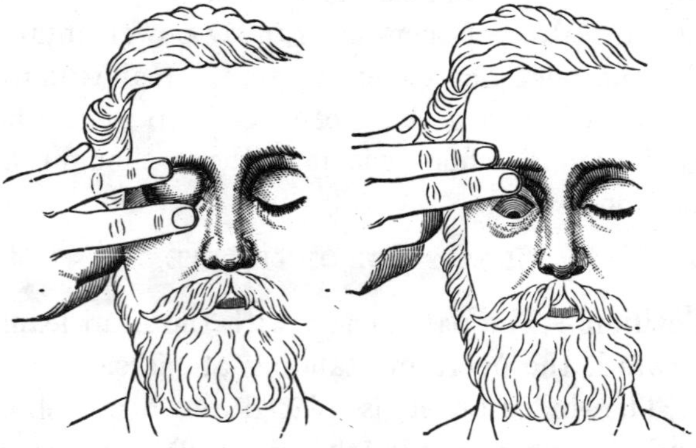

Fig. 25.—Massage of the Eye.

Stroke with two fingers on one side and the thumb on the other side of the trachea. Finish with similar stroking in connection with a slight shaking.

For the position of the hands in the vibration of the trachea and its surrounding tissues see Fig. 36, on page 58.

XIV. MASSAGE OF THE NECK

Position.—The patient faces the masseur (see Fig. 27) with the head thrown back, so as to expose the neck. The operator places his hands at the lobes

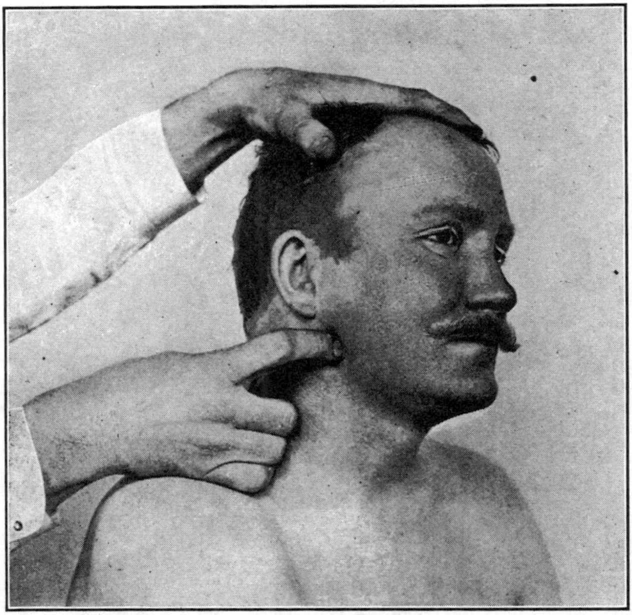

FIG. 26.—Avoid Pressure on the Jugular Vein.

of the ears and performs a stroking downward to the shoulder. The patient should be told to breathe freely and easily. This method (originated by Dr. Gerst) is used principally to increase the circulation in the veins of the neck.

Another method of massage of the neck has been recommended by *Hoeffinger*. The patient is sitting with the head erect. The operator stands behind and places his hands underneath the patient's

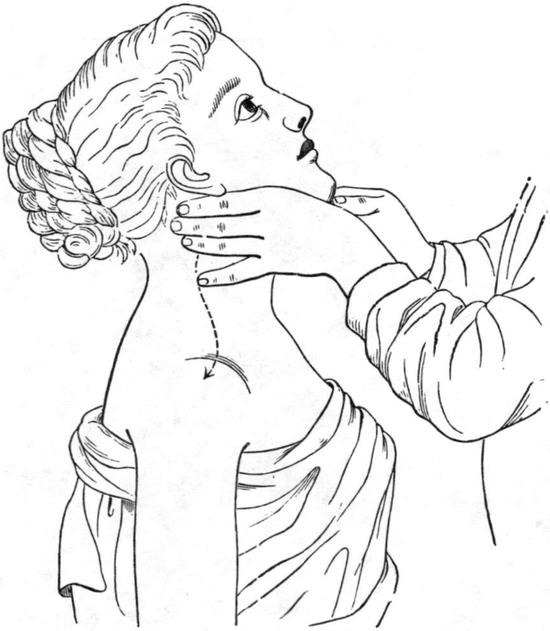

FIG. 27.—Massage of the Neck, Gerst's Method.

ears. The stroking is performed downward toward the shoulder, the hand covering the principal part of the trapezius (see Fig. 28).

I have often found frictions, kneadings and hacking of the neck (see Figs. 29, 30 and 31) of the greatest benefit, especially in cases of congestions and headaches, as recommended by Reibmayer.

XV. MASSAGE OF THE NOSE

Position.—The patient reclining.

The forefinger of each hand of the operator

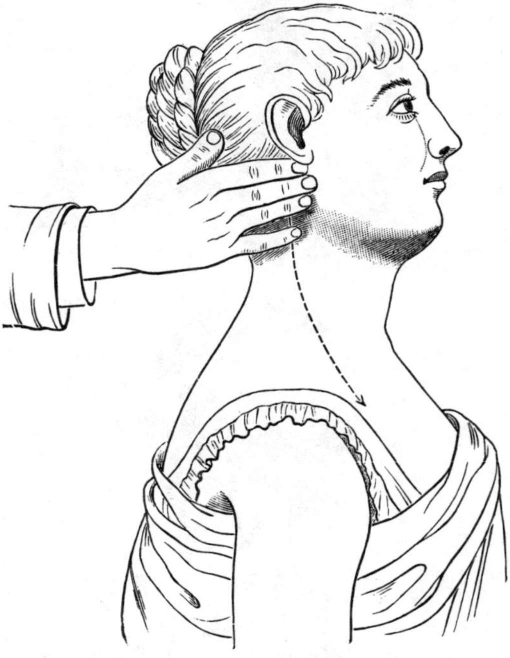

FIG. 28.—Massage of the Neck, Hoeffinger's Method.

is applied, with mild pressure, to each side of the nose, of the patient. A stroking downward is slowly and carefully performed.

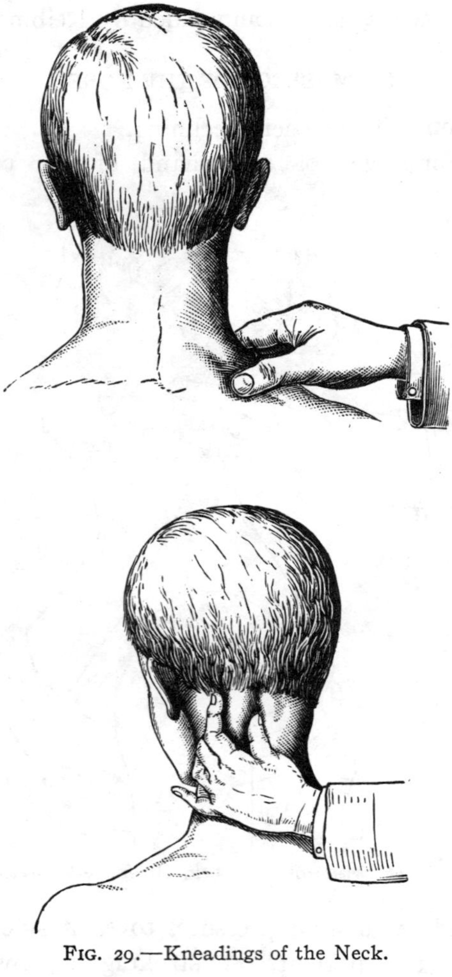

FIG. 29.—Kneadings of the Neck.

In removing scars on or near the nose stretch the part and work crosswise, as described under massage of the face.

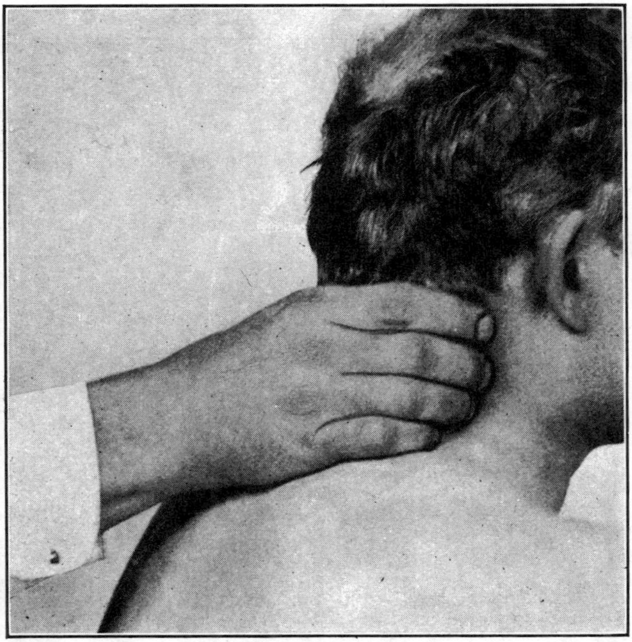

FIG. 30.

XVI. MASSAGE OF THE OVARIES

Position.—The patient should be flat on her back without head-rest and the knees drawn up so as to completely relax the abdomen.

1. Stroking with both hands. The operator

stands with her back to the patient placing her hands near the crests of the ilium, stroke simultaneously with both hands downward and inward to the center.

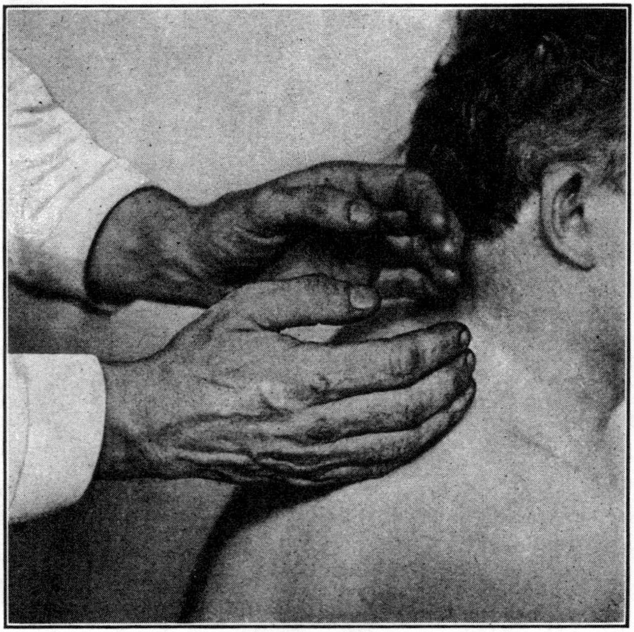

FIG. 31.

2. Friction with the tips of the fingers. This manipulation is used particularly when we wish to break down adhesions.

The patient should be instructed to breathe deeply. Massage of the ovaries is freely recommended by European gynecologists and we have many remarkable reports of complicated cases successfully treated. Gynecologic massage should not be practised by a non-medical man.—[*Editor*.]

XVII. MASSAGE OF THE UTERUS

Position.—The same as for massage of the abdomen (see Fig. 19, page 31).

The *external method* is merely a modification of the massage of the abdomen. The patient must be in a half lying position, with the knees flexed in order to relax the abdominal muscles. Begin with the circular manipulations, from right to left, following with *stroking* and *friction* over the lower part of the abdomen.

It is generally used for atony of the uterine organs, and must always be succeeded by *percussion* or *beating* of the lower part of the back. The Swedish movements are a valuable auxiliary, controlling as they do, the circulation in the abdomen and the lower extremities. The massage increases the current in the blood-vessels and the lymphatics, the resorption is restored, and the muscular organs in the smaller pelvis are strengthened.

Special manipulation of the intestines relieve the bowels, which in cases of uterine affections must be of great importance.

2. A *second method* is rather difficult to perform, as one or two fingers must be inserted in the vagina or the rectum, against which we work from

the outside. It should be performed only by a person who has a thorough knowledge of the parts; in fact it belongs to the practice of the gynecologist alone. Dr. Homer C. Bloom, of Philadelphia, has written a valuable little pamphlet on "Pelvic Massage." He describes the treatment and furnishes reports of some few cases. There is one part which is particularly interesting to every scientific masseur. Dr. Bloom, after summarizing the results, says: "It has been noticed that, in a great number of these cases, there was a concomitant condition of hemorrhoids, which were relieved in *every* instance."

Dr. Norstrom, in Paris, recommends in massage of the uterus:

1. Graduate the pressure of the uterine body after you have seized it.

2. In order to get a good hold, push down during expiration; maintain the distance gained during inspiration and start again during the next expiration.

3. Be careful not to increase by any sudden movements, the painful impression experienced by the patient when the uterus is first taken hold of; wait a moment before beginning pressure. The pressure sometimes produces reflex pains in various parts of the body.

4. Devote all your attention to supporting the uterus. This is easy when it is large and soft; very difficult when it is small and hard; it is then that it moves with great facility to one side or the other.

Any one specially interested in uterine massage will find a great deal of valuable information in a book published by Dr. Rob. Ziegenspeck, of Münich, and translated into English by Dr. F. H. Westerschulte, of Chicago. In this book Major Thure Brandt's methods are carefully analyzed and illustrated.

XIII. MASSAGE OF THE PROSTATE GLAND

Two methods are used, one external and one internal. In the first the patient is placed flat on his back, holding himself, the reproductive organs stretched up on the abdomen. The perineum is massaged with strokings and frictions.

In the other method the operator inserts his covered middle or if necessary index- and middle-finger, with some lubricant on the finger, cold cream or pure fresh lard, in the patient's rectum; and fixing the gland he supports it from the inside while the thumb and the fingers of the other hand perform the manipulations. The bladder should always be evacuated before beginning the treatment.

Some forms of vibrations have proved very useful, particularly when applied through the rectum internally.

PRESSING AND SHAKING (VIBRATIONS)

Closely connected with the massage proper are the oscillatory movements,—which we call *vibrations*,—used principally upon the extremities and over some of the internal organs.

We have two principal forms of vibrations—viz., *digital*, with one or more fingers; *palmar*, with the palm of the hand. In digital vibration the operator uses his fingers in vertical motion over a nerve or separate organ, no flexion or extension of the hand being allowed, as too heavy pressure will then be made. "The straining of the muscles in the operator's arm ought to be so slight as to be scarcely perceptible to any one who has his hand over them."

In Fig. 32 we have represented a digital vibration of the forearm. Vibration of the whole *arm* is given in the following manner: The operator grasps the hand and shoulder, keeping the arm in an extended position, and shakes as quickly as possible. The movement may also be performed by two operators.

In vibration of the *leg* the operator grasps the foot with one hand and the thigh, as high as possible, with the other, he raises the limb up and shakes it quickly.

In Fig. 33 we have demonstrated the palmar

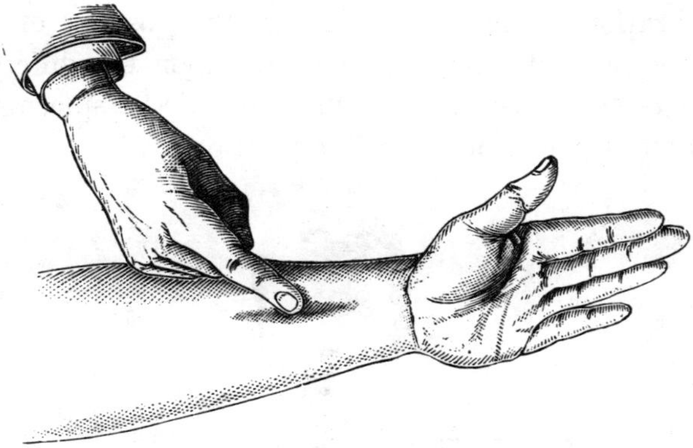

FIG. 32.—Digital Vibration.

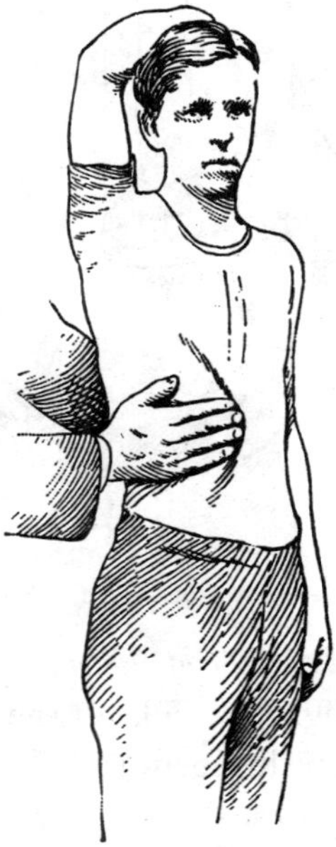

FIG. 33.—Vibration of the Liver.

vibration of the liver. Change the position of the hand several times, so as to act upon the different parts of the organ. In vibration of the spleen the hand is placed in a similar position.

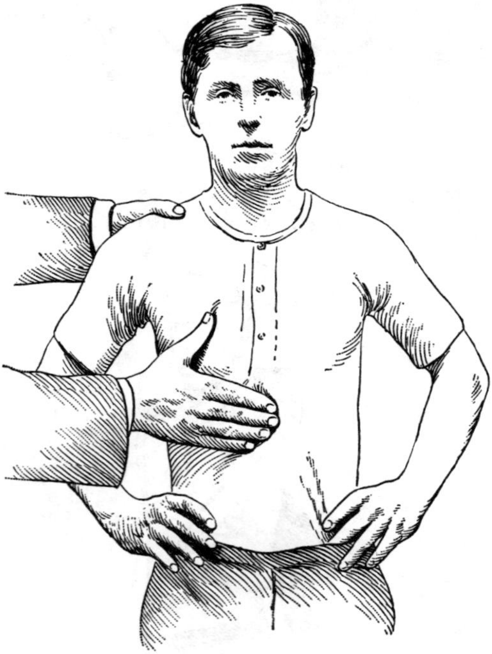

FIG. 34.—Vibration over the Solar Plexus.

Vibration at the *pit of the stomach* is clearly demonstrated in Fig. 34. Place the finger-tips about two inches below the ensiform cartilage and perform the shaking backward and upward. The patient may also stand with his hands clasped at the back of his head. This form of vibration is exceedingly useful in certain affections of the stomach. It also acts strongly upon the solar plexus.

Pressing and shaking of the *bladder*. The patient is lying flat on his back with knees drawn up so as to

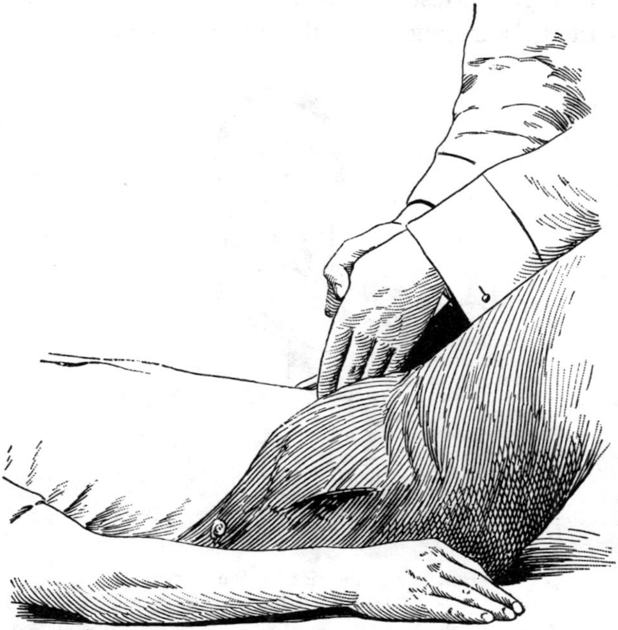

FIG. 35.—Vibration over the Bladder.

relax the abdominal muscles. The operator stands at his side, as in Fig. 35, and with his fingers he performs a gentle pressure and quick vibrations. Used in affections of the bladder and the prostate gland with modifications, also in uterine and rectal troubles.

Vibration of the *larynx* is shown in Fig. 36. The thumb is placed on one side of the thyroid cartilage and the fingers on the other. It should be performed gently at first until the patient becomes used to it.

In Fig. 37 we show the vibration of the *eyes*. The patient is sitting with the back supported. The

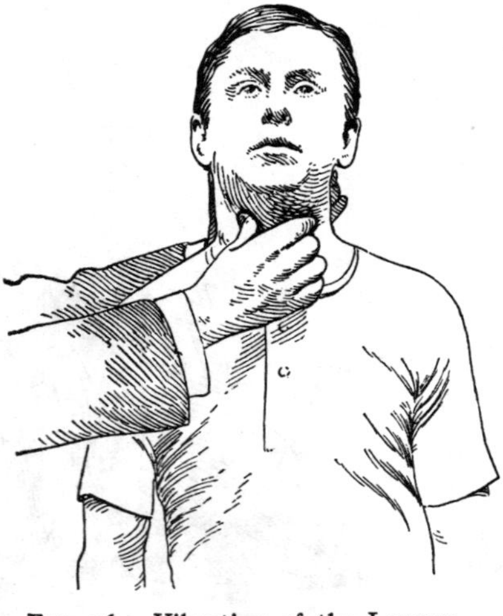

FIG. 36.—Vibration of the Larynx.

operator stands behind and places two fingers over each eye. The lids should not move up and down, but be kept steady, as the vibration is generated through them.

Vibrations are also used over the pharynx, the thorax (one hand on each side generally) the head, the heart and different parts of the abdomen. The author frequently uses the vibration of the descending colon and over the sigmoid flexure with the most excellent results.

Pressing and shaking have a stimulating and strengthening effect upon the nerves; they also act

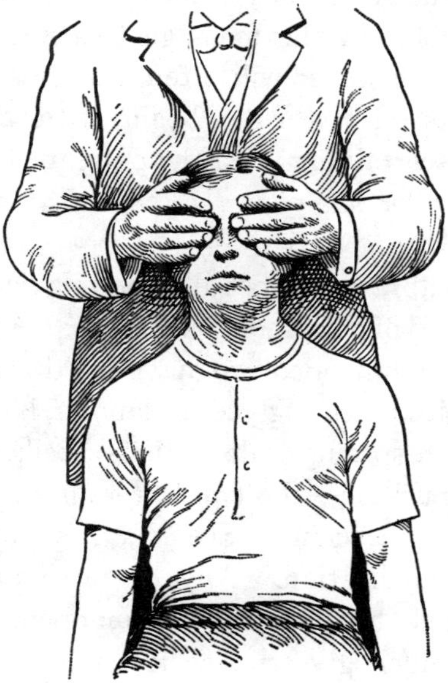

FIG. 37.—Vibration of the Eyes.

strongly upon the circulation of the venous blood-vessels and the lymphatics.

Kellgren's "Technic of Manual Treatment" is an interesting book on the subject of vibrations in general and their therapeutic indications.

DETAILS OF TREATMENT

The strength of the various manipulations is a principal point in the massage treatment, and the "self-made" masseur will often unnecessarily bruise his patients. As a rule, begin with a moderate pressure, ascertaining from the patient his sensation. *A new operator has often the fault of using too much pressure.*

To avoid abrasions most all Scandinavian operators use some kind of oleaginous substance. Among preparations recommended we have used with advantage: White vaselin, glycerin, lanolin, lard, olive oil, arnica oil (in sprains or distortions), belladonna ointment (in neuritis),—the two latter only when recommended by physicians. See Neuritis, page 135, for additional medication. Any of these preparations may be used, but I would caution operators against using too much glycerin, as it tends to irritate the skin. In America cocoanut-oil or cocoa-butter has been freely used.—Pure cold cream is one of the best lubricants and almost always at hand in every home. White vaselin, on the contrary, becomes after a few massage strokes very sticky; lard does not keep well, but is good when fresh; melted cocoa-butter answers the purpose also.—[*Editor*.]

Some physicians and patients object to using

grease of any kind. It is not my intention to advise operators to use large quantities of fat, but just enough to make the manipulations smoothly. On very hairy persons it is absolutely necessary to use some kind of grease.

All grease must be well rubbed off the skin before leaving the patient. The operator should wash his hands before and after every treatment; if necessary, use some antiseptic.

Every part should be well covered after masséeing it.

MASSAGE MUST ALWAYS BE APPLIED ON THE NUDE SKIN

The masseur who works outside the clothes, when acting upon special parts of the body, "works in the dark," tires his fingers, and loses a principal feature in the application—the *feeling*, which is so extremely necessary in a careful masseur. Some authors claim that working outside the clothes will save the patient's skin; but could anything be more pleasant and agreeable than a soft hand?

CONTRAINDICATIONS FOR MASSAGE

In several affections massage is most certainly contraindicated; and in many the treatment must be performed very carefully.

The first important requisite is that the skin is not severely abraded. Consequently, massage is not to be used in—

1. *Skin affections:* Wounds, burns, erysipelas, eczema, acne, and specific eruptions.

2. *Certain Affections in the Blood-vessels or Lymphatics.*—This must be especially remembered in elderly persons, whose vessels are, as a rule, very sensitive to mechanical pressure.

3. *In tumors and purulent inflammations*, in which we run the risk of transferring the virus to other healthy tissues.

4. *In all acute affections of the bone-tissue.*

5. *In severe constitutional or local diseases*, where complete rest is necessary. (When convalescent, massage, is, on the contrary, in many cases, one of the best tonics.)

6. *Pregnancy.*—As a rule, avoid massage during pregnancy, and especially massage of the abdomen.

7. *All affections* in which the pressure is liable to cause a hemorrhage.

During menstruation it is best to discontinue general massage, and under no circumstances should the abdomen be treated unless so ordered by the attending physician. Such prescriptions will sometimes be issued in cases of a retarded or too scanty flow.

SWEDISH MOVEMENTS

The Swedish Movements are a series of systematic exercises therapeutically applied to the human body.

"*Every exercise the direction and the duration of which are fixed is a movement.*"

That is the definition of a movement given to us by the Swede, P. H. Ling, who lived and worked in the early part of the last century. He erected the first system of scientific movements, as before his time no approach had been made to a method of designating and classifying the positions and various movements of the body for the purposes contemplated in the MOVEMENT CURE.

In every science terminology is necessary; so even in this. Ling gave every movement a complicated or double name, the first part of which indicated the position which the patient must assume, the second part telling the nature of the movement itself; for instance, sitting, rotation of the arms.

Thus it is left to us to first analyze the *positions* and afterward the *movements*.

POSITIONS

Movements may be given or performed in many different positions of the body. It is necessary to have a *commencing*, *intermediate* and *terminating* position. Ling said that to render any movement definite and exact, a point of departure, a point of termination, and the line through which the body or any of its parts must pass, are to be clearly determined, as well as the rhythm of the action itself.

There are in Ling's system five principal or fundamental positions—viz.:

1. STANDING,
2. SITTING,
3. LYING,
4. KNEELING,
5. SUSPENDING OR HANGING.

Standing.—In this position, the legs, trunk, and head are erect. The heels should be together and the feet should form right angles. The arms should be kept at sides (see Fig. 38).

Sitting.—In this position the buttocks and the posterior part of the thigh rest against the chair or sofa. The legs, close together, form right angles with the thighs. The trunk and head should be erect (see Fig. 39).

Kneeling.—The body rests upon the knees and the anterior part of the legs. The feet should be kept outside of the supporting part, as demonstrated in Fig. 40.

Lying.—In this position, the patient's body rests against the sofa or bed with the head, the back and the legs (see Fig. 41).

Suspending.—In this position the patient is to grasp a horizontal bar that is elevated so that the feet do not touch the floor. There should be the

FIG. 38.—Standing Position.

FIG. 39.—Sitting Position.

FIG. 40.—Kneeling Position.

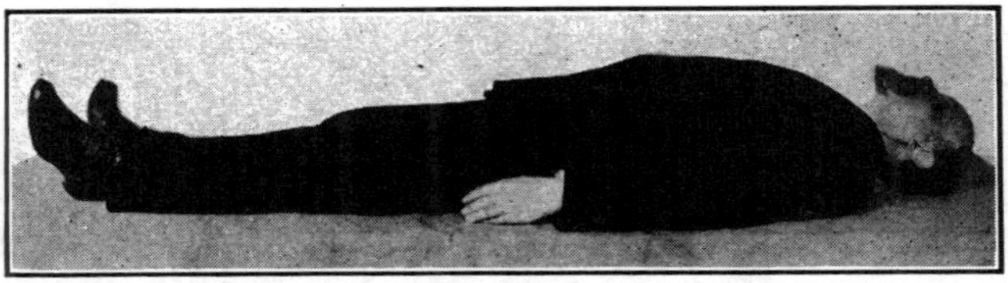

FIG. 41.—Lying Position.

same distance between the hands on the bar as between the shoulders (see Fig. 42). The position is very tiresome, as it, to a certain extent prevents respiration and circulation, on account of the extension of the thorax. It should be used with great care; and if the patient is weak, support his sides until he becomes accustomed to it.

FIG. 42.—Suspending Position.

From each one of these principal positions Ling formed many *derivatives* or subdivisions of positions.

We only mention the most important, and the illustrations will enable the reader to fully understand them.

DERIVATIVE POSITIONS FROM THE STANDING POSITION

1. With the Lower Extremities.

FIG. 43.—Flex-Standing.

FIG. 44.—Little Knee-bend.

FIG. 45.—Walk-Standing.

FIG. 46.—Side-Standing.

FIG. 47.—Side-Flex-Standing.

FIG. 48.—Balance-Standing.

FIG. 49.—Fall-Out-Standing.

2. With the Upper Extremities.

FIG. 50.—Bent-Standing.

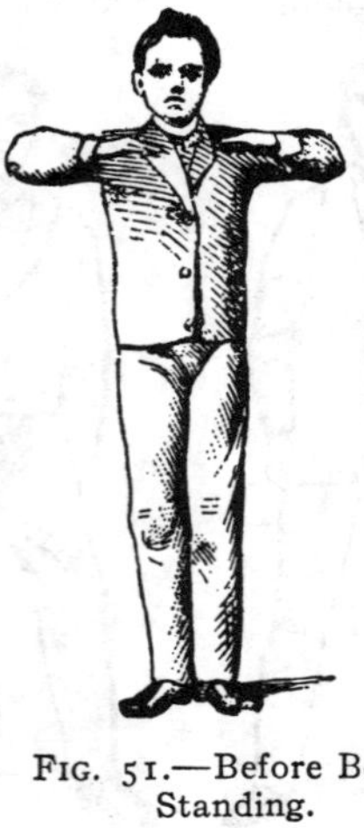

FIG. 51.—Before Bent Standing.

FIG. 52.

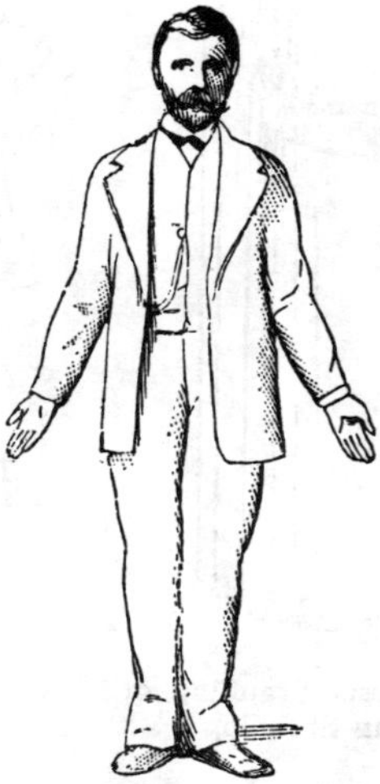
FIG. 53.—Talk-Standing.

FIG. 54.—Arm Stretched Standing.

FIG. 55.—Wing-Standing.

FIG. 56.—Think-Standing.

FIG. 57.—Resist-Standing, or Arm-lean Standing.

FIG. 58.—Rest-Standing.

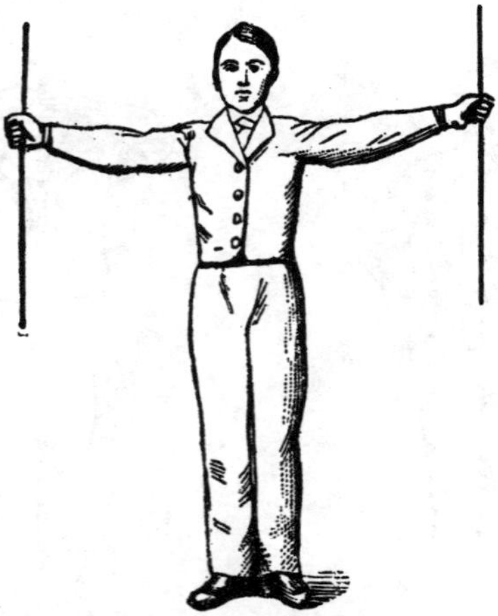

FIG. 59.—Yard-Standing.

3. With the Trunk.

FIG. 60.—Curve-Standing.

FIG. 61.—Turn-Standing.

FIG. 62.—Stoop-Curve-Standing.

DERIVATIVE POSITIONS FROM THE SITTING POSITION

1. With the Lower Extremities.

FIG. 63.—Long-Sitting.

FIG. 64.—Half-Long-Sitting.

FIG. 65.—Straddle-Sitting.

FIG. 66.—Short-Sitting.

2. With the Trunk.

Fig. 67.—Fall-Sitting.

DERIVATIVE POSITION FROM THE KNEELING POSITION

Fig. 68.—Side-Kneeling.

DERIVATIVE POSITIONS FROM THE LYING POSITION

See Fig. 19. Page 31. (Crook-lying.)

The subdivisions of positions here mentioned have given rise to a difficult terminology, as in many of them no equivalent English word can be found. They are, however, of great importance

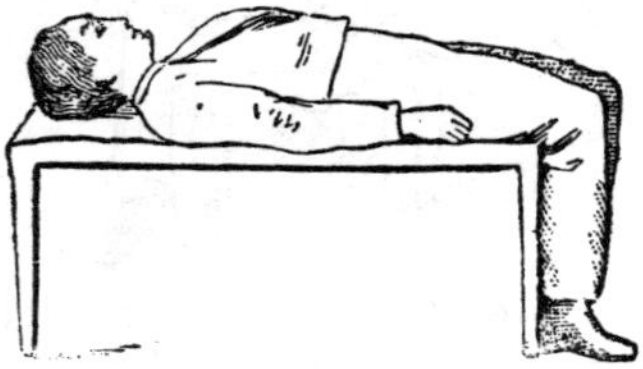

FIG. 69.—Sit-lying.

to everybody who contemplates practising Swedish movements, and as to their practical use we will refer to them in connection with the movements.

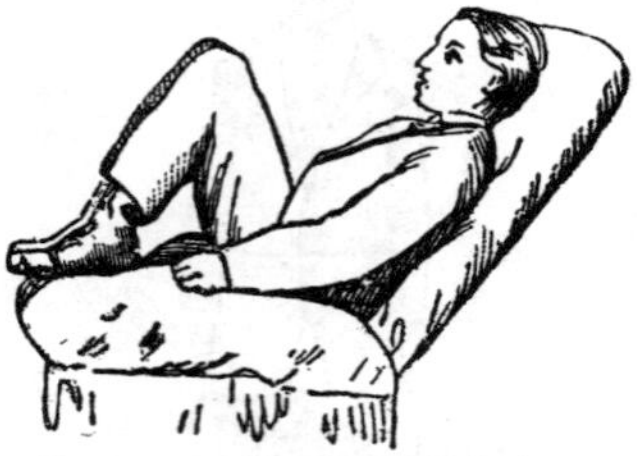

FIG. 70.—Crook-Half-Lying.

Only a few examples of their importance will be given here. In the derivative positions of standing with the arms, we can act upon certain parts or temporarily prevent certain organs or tissues from performing their functions. In the positions demonstrated in Figs. 48, 52, 54, 56, the chest is considerably expanded, which causes deeper inspirations.

In cases of "round shoulders," "narrow chest," etc., it is of great importance to select the proper one of these derivative positions for the movement that is to be used.

DIVISION OF MOVEMENTS

Ling and his pupils divided the movements into:

1. Single.
2. Double.

The single movements they again subdivided into *passive* and *active*, and the double movements into *concentric* and *excentric*.

Passive movements *are such as are applied to the patient without his assistance.* (They may be performed by an operator, by a machine, or through the power of gravity.)

Active movements *are performed by the patient.*

Concentric (*active-passive*) *movements are performed by the patient, while the operator or some other power resists.*

Excentric (*passive-active*) *movements are performed by some power outside of the patient, while he resists.*

The principal difference between the *concentric* and *excentric* movements is that in the former the muscle is shortened, in the latter it is stretched. As to their nature and physiologic action, it is easy to understand that they are but little different from the single active movements. *Practically they are of great use, as by them we are able to exactly fix the amount of mechanical work done by the patient in each movement.*

To make the terminology somewhat simpler for the reader, we have in the description of the movements used the expression *duplicated active* movements, by that covering both concentric and excentric movements in the Ling system.

THE VARIOUS MOVEMENTS

1. Rotation.
2. Flexion and Extension.
3. Separating and Closing.
4. Bending.
5. Raising.
6. Pulling.
7. Turning.
8. Depression and Elevation.

1. ROTATION

Rotation is a circular movement by which the different joints are brought into motion within their natural limits.

I. **Rotation of the feet** may be performed with the patient in a sitting or half-lying position.

In the first position, the operator sits in front of the patient and, taking the feet in his lap, grasps the toes and moves the feet outward, describing a circle. In the second position, the patient is half-lying, his feet resting on the couch or bed. The operator grasps the toes and proceeds with the same motion as above. Relax the muscles, if necessary, by shaking the toes.

The rotation of the feet is intended to promote circulation in the lower extremities and is often used for attracting the blood from other parts. The movement is performed fifteen to thirty times. The strength of the motion depends upon the size of the circle described. (Passive.)

II. **Rotation of the Foot.**—The operator, sitting in front of the patient, takes the heel in his left hand and grasping the toes with the right, performs a rotatory motion from the ankle, pressing the foot forward. Ten to fifteen times in each series. It is used principally for deformities and affections of the feet. (Passive.)

III. **Rotation of the Leg.**—The patient is in a half-lying position. The operator, placing one hand on the sole of the foot and the other below the knee, with the thumbs inward, raises the leg and performs a circular motion by the hip-joint, pressing upward, inward and outward. Twelve to fifteen times on each limb. It is used to regulate the circulation of the abdominal organs and to prevent stiffness in the hip-joint. (Passive or Active.)

IV. **Rotation of the Arms.**—The patient sitting. The operator, standing behind, grasps the extended arms below the elbows and rotates them upward and outward. The patient may also be in a standing position, in which case the operator must support him with his chest. It is used principally to assist respiration and circulation. (Passive or Active.)

V. **Rotation of the Shoulder.**—The patient sitting or standing. The operator, putting one hand on the shoulder-joint and the other below the elbow, rotates upward and outward. Fifteen to twenty times. The movement is used for stiffness in the joint and for inflammation of certain muscles. (Passive.)

VI. **Rotation of the Hand.**—The operator takes the patient's hand, and, grasping the wrist with his free hand, rotates from side to side. Ten to eighteen times. It is used for stiffness in the wrist after fractures of the arm; also to increase the circulation. (Passive.)

VII. **Rotation of the Head.**—The patient sitting with the back supported. The operator, placing one hand on the forehead and the other on the neck, rotates SLOWLY from side to side. Eight to ten times. It is used for anemia of the brain, stiffness of the neck, and insomnia, etc. (Passive.)

VIII. **Rotation of the Body.**—The patient in a sitting position, with hands on hips. The operator standing behind, places his right hand on the right shoulder-blade, and his left in front, on the chest of the left side, and performs the motion in such a way as to press the patient forward with one hand and carry him backward with the other, always being careful to describe a circle. When the movement is performed to one side ten to fifteen times, change the position of the hands and rotate toward the other side. It is used principally for affections of the abdomen. To secure a very strong action of the movement, the patient turns his body somewhat in the motion. (Passive.)

IX. **Rotation of the Pelvis.**—The patient resting with body on a couch or bed, and grasping it to keep immovable, the lower extremities extended. The operator grasps the feet and proceeds with the rota-

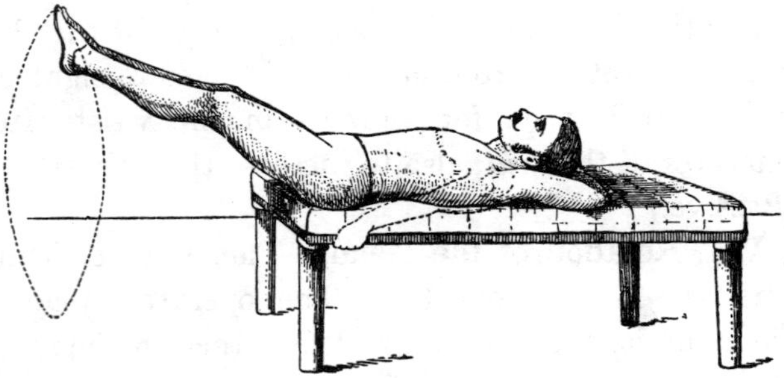

FIG. 71.

tion of the legs, endeavoring to produce a circle large enough to bring the pelvis into action.

Rotate ten times to each side, if the patient's strength permits. (Passive.)

This movement may also be active and is performed as in Fig. 71.

The aim of the rotation is to lengthen and shorten the veins, so as to produce a sucking of their contents, thus stimulating the circulation and assisting the heart in its action.

2. FLEXION AND EXTENSION

I. **Foot.**—The patient lying or sitting. The operator, grasping the ankle with one hand and the toes with the other, moves the foot up and down as far as the limits of the joint permit. Ten to eighteen times. It is used for deformities, and especially for stiffness of the Achilles tendon. (Passive and Duplicated Active.)

The movement may also be performed on both feet at the same time, as demonstrated in Fig. 72.

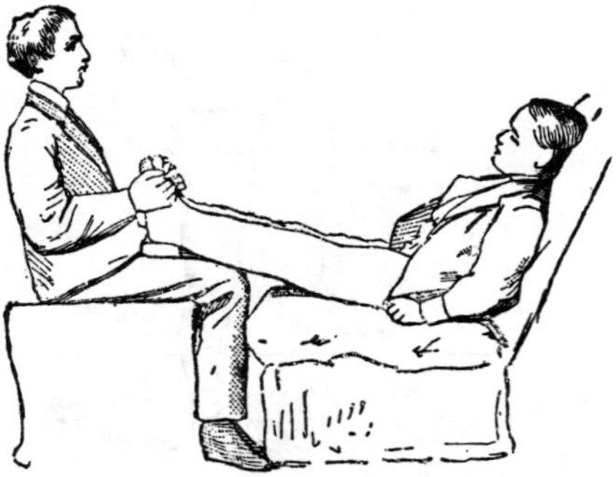

FIG. 72.—Flexion and Extension of the Feet.

II. **Leg.**—The patient is in half-lying (see Figs. 75 and 76) or standing (see Fig. 74) position. The operator places one hand at the knee, the other either on top of the instep or underneath the sole of the foot.

The patient generally moves the limb up and down while the operator resists. (Duplicated Active.)

It may also be a passive movement, and is used for

stiffness in the knee and hip-joint, and for contraction of certain muscles.

In Fig. 73 we have demonstrated the single active, standing flexion and extension of the leg. Until the patient gets used to the exercise, it is safest to have him grasp something to support himself and prevent him from falling. The effect of this movement is not confined to the extremity only, but the abdominal muscles are strongly and effectively acted upon. It is therefore very valuable in the treatment of constipation and hemorrhoids.

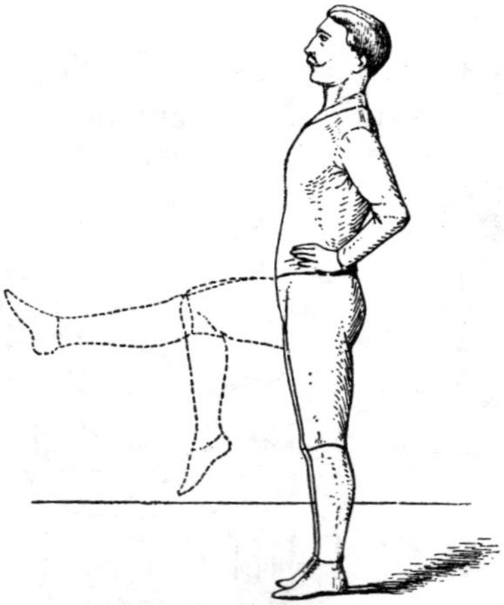

FIG. 73.—Standing Flexion and Extension of the Leg.

III. **Arms.**—The patient sitting. The operator, standing behind, grasps the patient's wrists, telling him to keep his elbows close to the body and to move the arms up and down, the operator making suitable resistance. Ten times. It is a circulatory movement. (Duplicated Active.)

IV. **Arm.**—The patient sitting. The operator, standing in front, grasping the wrist with one hand and around the triceps muscle with the other, the patient moves the arm up and down, the operator making suitable resistance. Ten to fifteen times.

FIG. 74.—Flexion and Extension of the Leg.

The motion may also be passive, and is used for acting upon the joints and for certain local affections. (Passive or Duplicated Active.)

V. **Hand.**—The patient sitting. The operator, in front, takes the fingers firmly in one hand, the other grasping the wrist, and works up and down, about ten times. It is used for stiffness of the wrist, sprains and for writer's cramp. (Passive or Duplicated Active.)

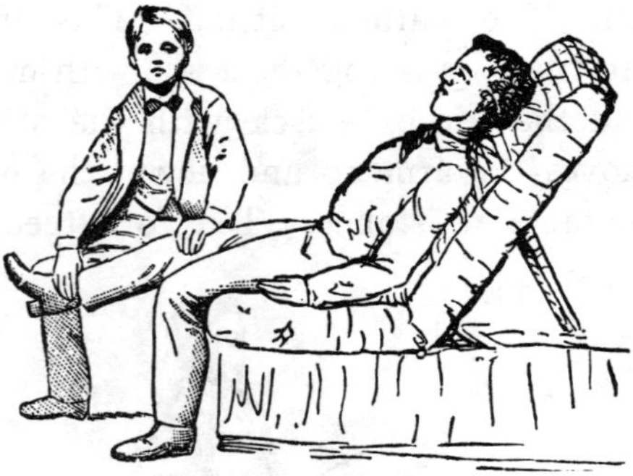

FIG. 75.

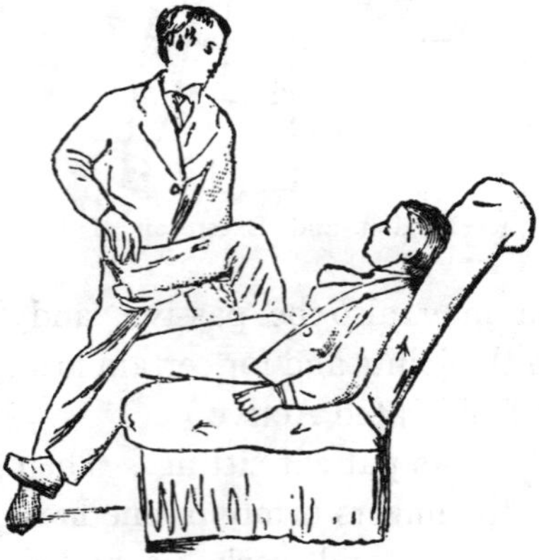

FIG. 76.

Flexion and extension are used principally for regulating the circulation in certain parts and for relieving local congestion.

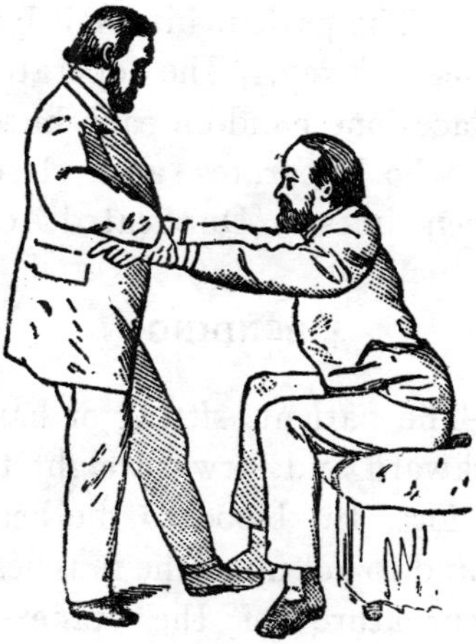

FIG. 77.

3. SEPARATING AND CLOSING

I. **Arms.**—The patient sitting with arms extended. The operator, standing in front, grasps his wrists; the patient moves his arms out and in, the operator resisting. It is used for expanding the chest and in spinal curvatures., (Duplicated Active.) (See Fig. 77.)

II. **Legs.**—The patient sitting, or half-lying. The operator grasps the ankles underneath, the patient separates and closes his legs; with the resistance of the operator, who may need an assistant. (Duplicated Active.)

This movement acts upon different abdominal organs.

III. **Knees.**—The patient in a half-lying position, with the knees flexed. The operator, standing at his side, places one hand on each knee and resists the patient, who separates and closes his legs. Eight to sixteen times. (Duplicated Active.)

4. BENDING

I. **Head.**—The patient, sitting or hanging, bends the head backward and forward eight to ten times. It is used to force the blood to the head in anemia of the brain, and to act upon the muscles of the back in lateral curvature of the spine. (Active or Duplicated Active.)

In Figs. 78 and 79, we have demonstrated the active bending of the head forward and backward, and to the sides respectively. These are used when we wish to draw the blood from the head in full blooded individuals or when we wish to develop the neck. The patient resists himself while performing the movement.

II. **Body** (sideways).—Suppose a case of lateral curvature of the spine. If the right side is the originally affected one, *i.e.*, right sided convexity, the patient stands with his left arm straight up, close to the head. The operator, standing behind,

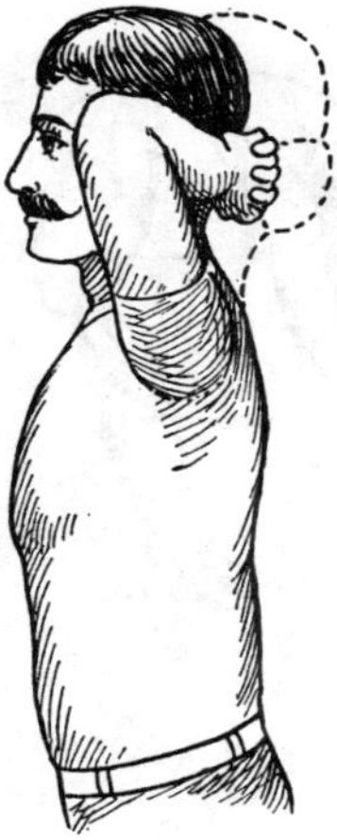

FIG. 78.

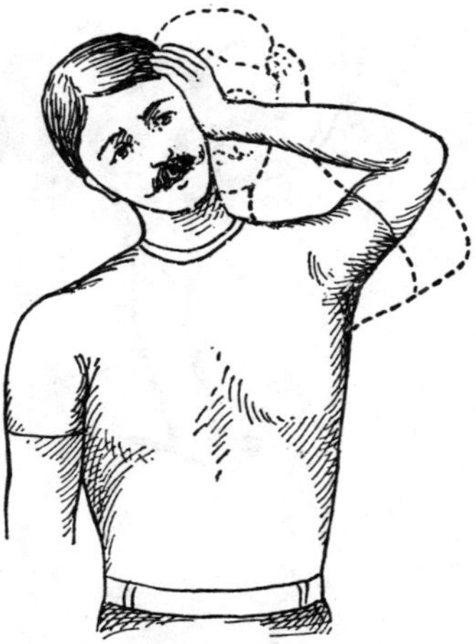

FIG. 79.

FIG. 80.

FIG. 81.

FIG. 82.

FIG. 83.

FIG. 84.

places one hand on the right side, at the highest point of curvature, the other on the opposite hip; the patient bends slowly toward the right side,

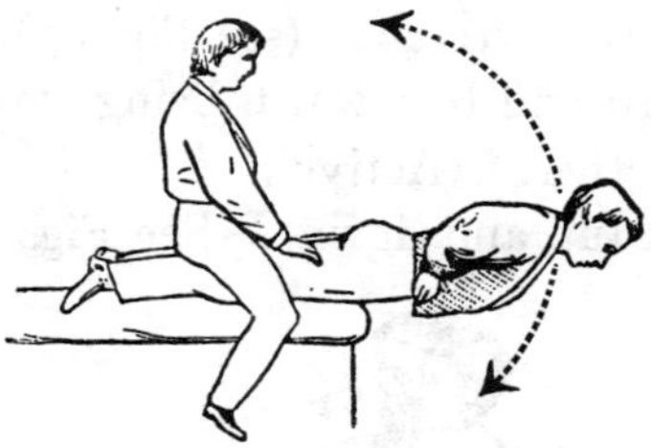

FIG. 85.

thus acting upon the affected muscles. The movement may also be single active, as shown in Fig. 80.

Bending of the body sideways may also be performed in a sitting position (see Fig. 81), or as a

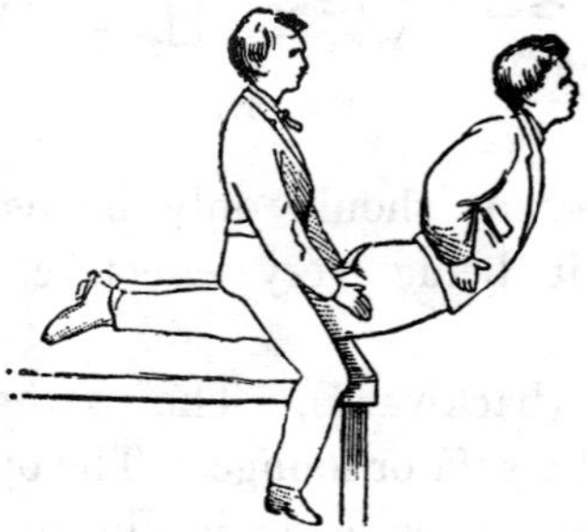

FIG. 86.

single active movement from side to side as shown in Fig. 84. This is particularly recommended when we wish to act upon the liver or spleen. It should be performed slowly, otherwise the patient is apt to become dizzy.

III. **Body** (forward and backward).—The patient is standing with the hands on hips (see Fig. 82) or with the arms stretched (see Fig. 83). He bends slowly forward and backward, being careful to keep the heels together. (Active.)

IV. **Trunk** (up and down).—See Figs. 85 and 86.

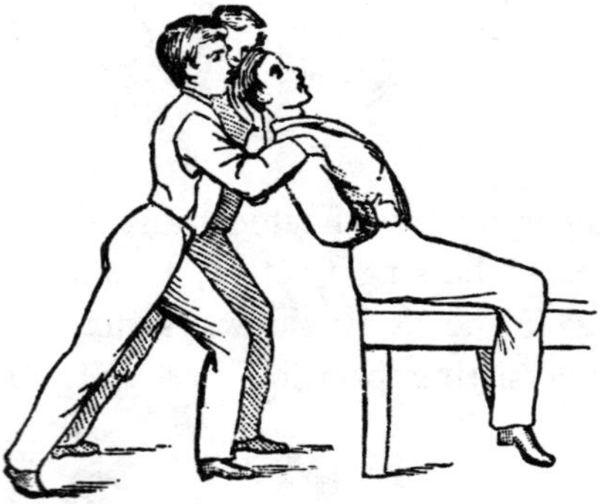

FIG. 87.

This movement should only be used on strong individuals, it being very effective. (Duplicated Active.)

V. **Trunk** (backward).—The patient is sitting at the edge of a sofa or lounge. The operators stand behind and support as shown in Fig. 87. The patient bends his trunk backward while the operators resist, and the patient resists while the operators raise him up.

The support should be made firm, so that the

patient feels confident in performing the movement. It is an excellent exercise to act upon the muscles of the back. (Duplicated Active.)

VI. **Knee.**—The operator stands behind the patient, as demonstrated in Fig. 88, and resists the patient rising. (Duplicated Active.)

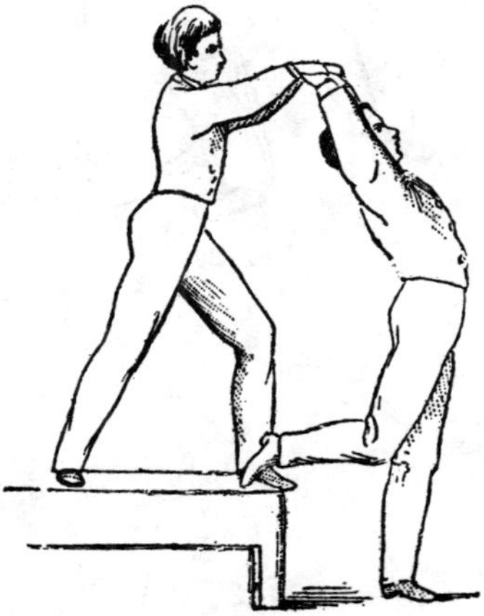

FIG. 88.

VII. **Knees.**—The patient stands with the hands on the back of his head or supported as in Fig. 89. The patient is told to rise on his tip-toes, flex his knees as much as possible, rise up on the tip-toes and to regain standing position. The operator supports either as shown in Fig. 89 or with one hand on the chest and the other on the back. It may also be single active as shown in Fig. 90. This movement is called "Deep Knee-Bend."

FIG. 89.

FIG. 90.

5. RAISING

I. **Leg.**—The patient lying on his back. The operator grasps the heel underneath, one hand supporting the knee on top and raises the extended leg upward. Ten times.

This movement may also be active and is used principally for sciatica and slight rupture.

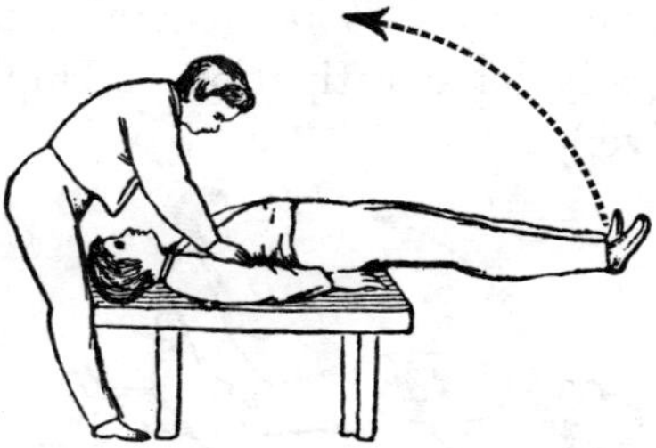

FIG. 91.

II. **Legs.**—The patient is lying flat on his back with the limbs extended as shown in Fig. 91. The operator grasps over the shoulders and presses the trunk down, while the patient raises the limbs upward far enough to have them form a right angle with the trunk at the hip. The movement acts firmly upon the abdomen. (Duplicated Active.)

III. **Body.**—The patient sitting on a stool or a turned chair. The operator places his hands flat on the shoulder-blade. The patient, if strong enough, clasps his hands on the back of his head and bends forward, keeping the head up. He then raises his body up, with a strong resistance of the operator.

It is used for deformities of the back. (Duplicated Active.)

IV. **Body.**—The patient lying with hands clasped on the back of his head. The operator places his hands around the ankles, with thumbs inverted, and holds them firmly. The patient then rises slowly to a sitting position. There is no better movement for compressing the contents of the bowels. The movement may also be general. active, and is used principally for constipation. (Duplicated Active or Active.)

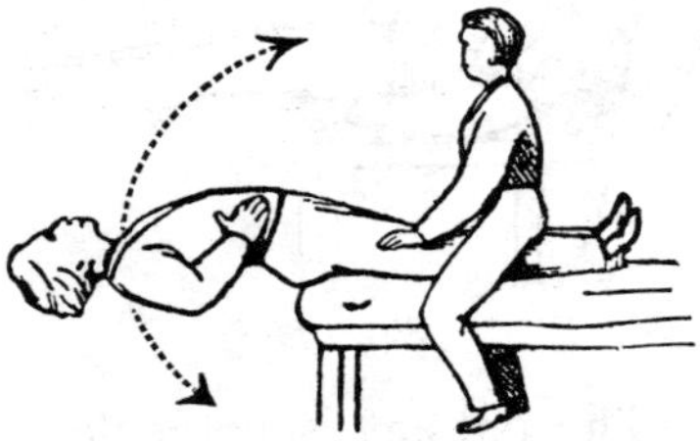

FIG. 92.

V. **Body.**—The movement may also be performed with the trunk extended from the lounge, as shown in Fig. 92. It is then very effective, and should be used with great consideration.

VI. **Body.**—Another form of raising the body in standing position is demonstrated in Fig. 94. The operator is sitting in front of the patient and resists him firmly in his rising. (Duplicated Active.)

Body.—The movement may also be performed as shown in Fig. 93. The patient is lying on a bed or couch the lower extremities out, feet on the floor

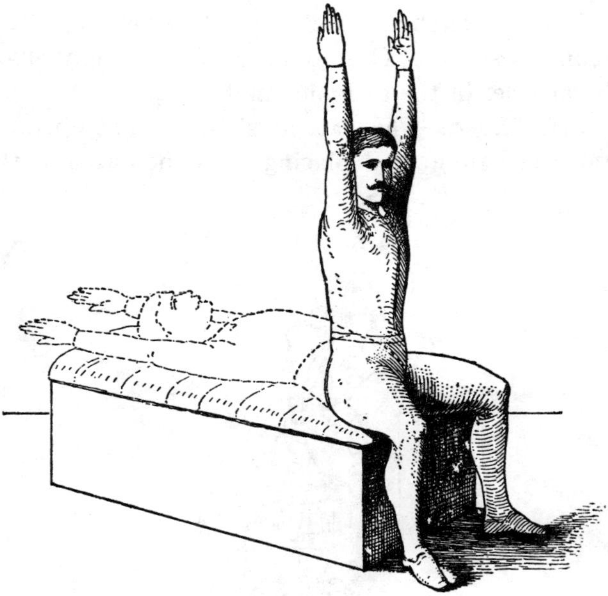

FIG. 93.

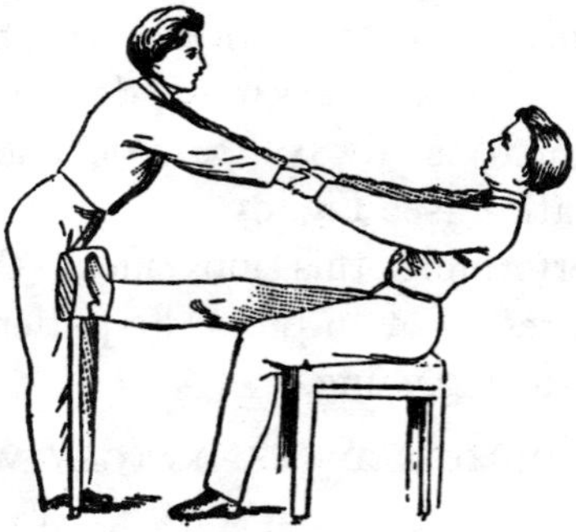

FIG. 94.

and arms stretched. He is told to slowly rise to a sitting position. This exercise acts strongly upon the muscles of the abdomen and chest.

VII. **Chest.**—The patient sitting. The operator standing behind and placing his hands around the

FIG. 95.

patient's armpits in front, raises the body slowly forward, upward and backward, describing a circle. This movement is always *passive*, and is used to assist respiration (see Fig. 95).

When performing this movement the operator should be careful not to press the patient too much forward in the beginning.

OSTROM'S COMBINED RESPIRATORY MOVEMENT

The patient stands erect with head thrown back and arms extended on a level with his shoulders.

1. Flex the arms slowly under slight resistance (single active), gentle inspiration.

2. Expiration.

3. Raise the flexed arms up so that the points of the elbows reach above the head, with deep inspiration.

4. Expiration while in this position.

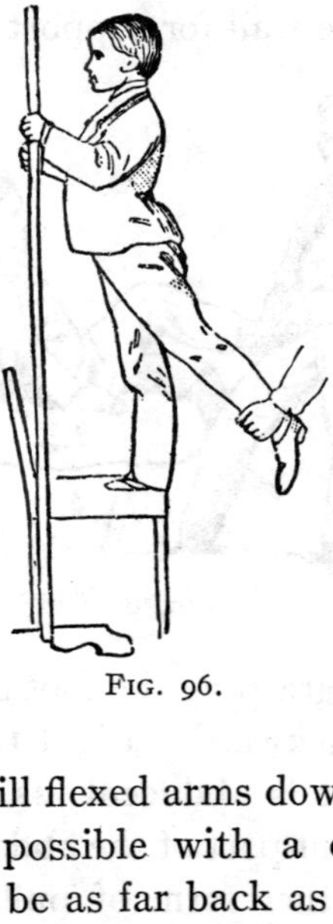

FIG. 96.

5. Bring the still flexed arms downward and backward as far as possible with a deep inspiration. The head should be as far back as possible so as to help expand the chest to its fullest capacity.

6. Expiration.

7. The arms are raised up on a level with the shoulders with deep inspiration.

8. The arms are extended back to their fundamental position slowly, while the patient exhales.

This movement is very strong and consequently rather tiresome to the patient. It should therefore be given carefully in the beginning.

6. PULLING

I. **Leg.**—The patient standing on a chair, with hands against the wall for support (see Fig. 96).

FIG. 97.

The operator, grasping the foot around the instep, carries the leg backward. Eight to fifteen times.

The movement is abducent, as it causes a great tension in the front part of the abdomen. (Passive.)

II. **Leg.**—Another form of pulling of the leg in sitting position is demonstrated in Fig. 97. The patient draws the limb upward with the operator's resistance; the operator pulls the limb down to the original position.

III. **Body** (backward).—The patient kneeling on the sofa, with knees separated; hands on hips. The operator stands behind, with one knee supporting the lumbar region, his hands grasping the armpits from behind, and carries the patient slowly backward (see Fig. 98); the latter making slight resistance. Six to twelve times, according to strength. (Duplicated Active.)

FIG. 98.

The movement has a strong effect upon the abdomen, and is used principally for case of painful menstruation.

IV. **Body.**—The position of operator and patient is shown in Fig. 99. The operator pulls the body backward, being careful to see that the bent position of the body is kept all through the movement.

7. TURNING

I. **Foot.**—The patient sitting or lying. The operator puts one hand back of the ankle, the other grasping the toes and the front of the foot, and turns the foot from side to side. The movement is always *passive*, and is used chiefly for sprains and deformities.

FIG. 99.

II. **Leg.**—The patient lying. The operator places one hand at the sole of the foot, the other pressing on the knee to keep the leg extended, thumbs inward, and moves the limb slowly inward and outward. The motion is used for stiffness in the hip joint and for contraction of certain muscles. (Passive.)

III. **Body.**—The patient standing (see Fig. 100) or sitting Fig. 101), with hands on the hips or clasped on the back of the head. The operator, standing behind, places his right hand on one shoulder and his left in front of the other, and moves the patient to one side and back again, changing the position of the hands before turning to the other side. The movement is also duplicated active, and is used for congestion of the abdominal organs and for acting upon its great venous system.

FIG. 100.

FIG. 101.

In Figs. 103, 104, 105 and 106 we have depicted certain modifications of turning of the body. The one shown in Fig. 106 should be used with great care, it being very effective, especially in the case of a woman.

Fig. 104 shows how the turning of the body is performed as a single active movement. It acts strongly upon the abdominal viscera, especially upon the liver. The patient should be told to take deep breaths while performing the exercise.

FIG. 102.

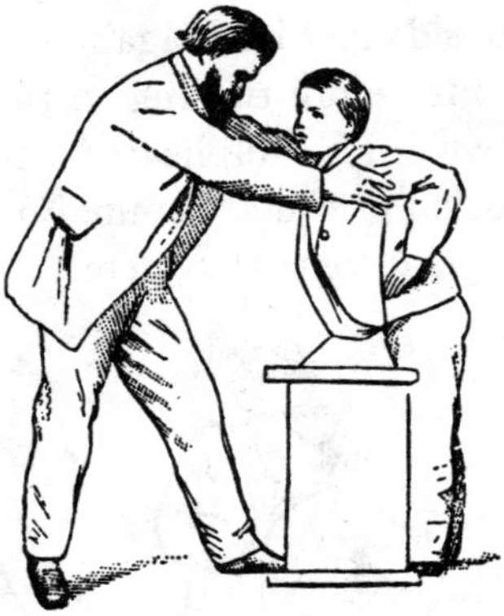

FIG. 103.

FIG. 104.

IV. **Arm.**—The patient sitting or standing. The operator, supporting the elbow with one hand and

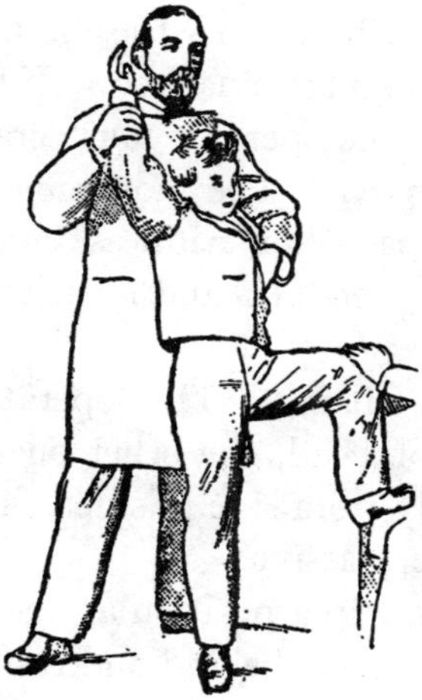

FIG. 105.

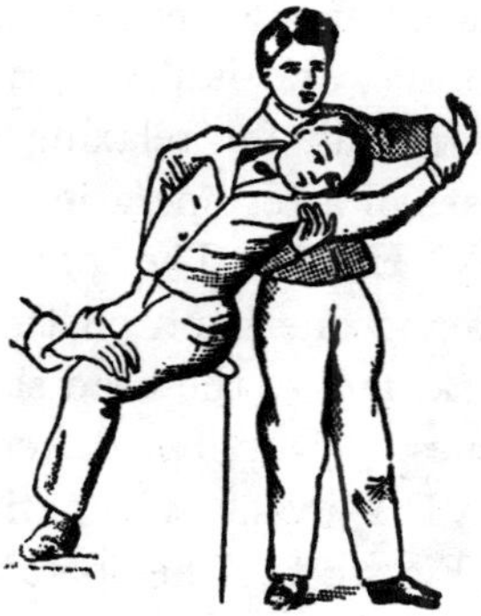

FIG. 106.

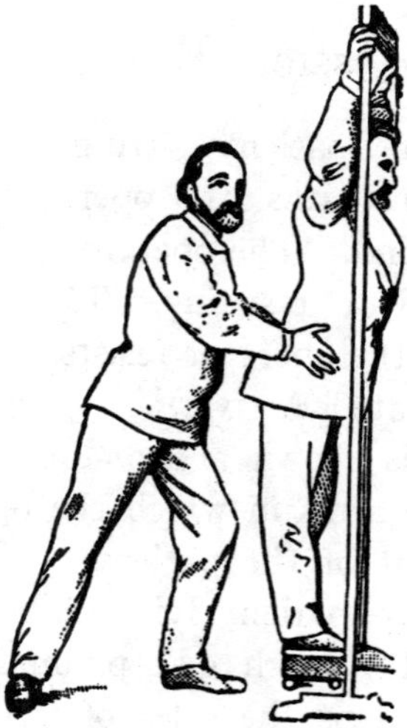

FIG. 107.

grasping the hand with the other, turns the forearm from side to side (pronation and supination). If the whole arm is to be turned, the operator must grasp the elbow to keep it extended. The movement is passive, and is used principally for stiffness in the joints and for relaxing the tendons and muscles in cases of after-operation.

V. **Head.**—The patient sitting. The operator, placing one hand on the forehead, the other on the neck, moves the head slowly from side to side. Ten times. (Duplicated Active, Passive.)

VI. **Pelvis.**—The patient is in a position as shown in Fig. 107. The operator stands behind and resists the patient in his turning forward and backward.

8. DEPRESSION AND ELEVATION

I. **Arms.**—The patient sitting or lying. The patient raises his arms, the operator grasping the hands from behind. The operator presses the arms down, the patient resisting. The patient raises the arms while the operator resists. Ten to twelve times. (Duplicated Active.)

In Fig. 108 is shown a form of depression and elevation of the arms in which the operator stands elevated in front of the patient.

II. **Legs.**—The patient lying flat on the back, grasping the bed or couch to keep himself immovable. The operator grasps the soles of the feet, thumbs inward. The movement is performed down and up with the knees turned out, the patient resisting in the elevation and the operator in the depression.

FIG. 108.

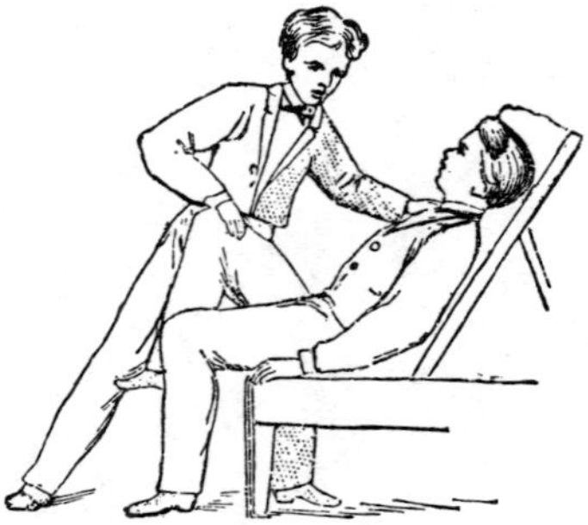

FIG. 109.

The movement is very effective and must be performed with great care. Six to ten times. (Duplicated Active.)

III. **Leg.**—In Fig. 109 we have demonstrated depression of the one leg, used for certain muscular affections in the thigh and around the pelvis.

Several movements belonging to the Swedish system have been omitted as not being of much practical use.

THE PHYSIOLOGY OF THE MOVEMENT TREATMENT

The **movement treatment** is not shrouded in mystery, nor is a minute knowledge of anatomy or physiology necessary to understand its nature and comprehend its workings. Its physiology is very simple and easily understood, because it always endeavors to follow the laws of nature.

Motion and activity are the principal characteristics of man; and all parts of the body are so formed as to fulfil their proper functions.

By the law of metamorphosis, every particle, after remaining a certain time in the body, is cast off, to be replaced by a new one. This alteration is carried on very slowly and almost imperceptibly, but without interruption.

Every one knows that it is impossible to abstain from food and not lose in weight and flesh. This loss indicates that the body is consuming itself, under a chemic process called *combustion*, by which heat is produced, and carbonic acid, water, etc., excreted by the lungs, the skin, the kidneys, and the intestines.

The process may be too rapid or too slow. The first takes place in fevers, with their high temperature and great emaciation; the second, in many chronic disorders, with lowered temperature and lowered vitality.

Those organs which are in a state of permanent activity are most likely to suffer from overwork; but there is danger of the opposite extreme in the muscular system, so much of which is dependent for action entirely upon the exercise of the will.

This great muscular system, with the nerves and vessels by which it is supplied, and the joints which it controls, comprises about nine-tenths of the whole organism.

Generally speaking, the action of the voluntary muscles is reduced to a *minimum*. How much of the great muscular system has the clerk brought into use? Only the muscles of the arm, the rest remaining inactive; and these muscles are so overtaxed as to cause an irritation of the nerves communicating with them, and the result is nervous disorders, such as writers' cramp.

Aside from what their occupation affords them (and that is more or less defective), most persons have no other exercise than the daily walk to and from their business, which rarely exceeds an hour a day. While this exercise is better than none, its benefits are often overestimated. In walking, only certain muscles are actively engaged, and even those very imperfectly. The muscles of the leg are used in taking the step and the muscles of the back in keeping the body upright, but this exercise, with its uniform nature, is of less value than any other.

It is necessary to give the muscles alternate work and rest. In walking, the muscles of the back are kept in a permanent state of tension, so that they have not the time perfectly to contract and relax, which is essential to beneficial exercise.

Although, from a purely hygienic standpoint walking in the pure air is of great benefit, aiding respiration, yet the daily walk to a given place becomes mechanical and automatic, no attention being paid to the movements by the will power.

It is evident to all that in the various motions of the body or the limbs a change is taking place in some of its tissues by means of *combustion.*

First, this activity creates heat, the intensity of which can be estimated, but not the amount. Second, a certain amount of waste material is thrown off and absorbed by the veins and the lymphatics, to be eventually excreted from the body. The creation of heat, which in a few minutes reaches several degrees, is soon made evident by copious perspiration.

The chemic change produces carbonic acid and other substances, which cause the feeling of languor. The sense of fatigue remains until the products of the change are carried away by the blood-vessels and the lymphatics.

By this process, which is constantly going on in the working muscles, some part of the tissue is consumed but the loss is compensated by the nourishment which it receives from the blood.

This exercise demands a greater supply of blood and neither its *quantity* nor its *quality* can be diminished without seriously endangering health.

To replenish the blood, the lymphatics carry the digested food (chyle) from the stomach and intestines into the blood-circulation. But before it is in a condition to nourish the body it must be carried to the great vessels of the lungs, when it is brought in contact with oxygen.

By proper exercise the respiratory movements become longer and deeper and the capacity of the lungs is very much increased.

The same stimulating effect is produced upon the circulatory system. An increased amount of blood is sent to the different parts, necessitating a freer circulation.

Thus we find that exercise systematically applied produces direct and positive action upon the *circulatory*, *digestive* and *respiratory* systems.

Since carbonic acid gas and water are carried off through the lungs and water and uric acid through the kidneys and skin, we can easily comprehend that exercise will aid materially in hastening the elimination of bodily waste.

Of course in the process of combustion heat is

necessarily produced, and if the excess is not carried off, serious results may ensue.

In health, nature has provided proper facilities for carrying off all heat above the normal amount by exhaustion from the skin and lungs.

MECHANICAL ACTION OF MUSCLES

There is also a mechanical process that takes place in every kind of muscular work, for when the muscle contracts, its mass is condensed, and the soft parts near the muscle are exposed to a very strong pressure.

This fact has a very important bearing upon the veins and the lymphatics, and upon the fluids which these vessels carry to the heart.

While the heart principally controls the action of these vessels, much aid is afforded them by the temporary pressure of the contracted muscles, and thus we see that exercise stimulates and increases the circulation in the veins and lymphatic vessels.

But these are not all the results that are produced by proper exercise. In voluntary muscular action, as a rule, one or two joints are set in motion.

These joints are protected, to prevent their bony surfaces from coming in contact with each other. While the motion is a rubbing or friction movement, exercise properly taken is free from all danger; moreover, the joint is decidedly benefited by such action, nutrition to the part being increased.

Generally, where the muscles are attached to the bones large *processes* or elevations are found; and the greater the muscles the larger the processes.

This must indicate an increased nutrition to the bone, as well as increased strength to the osseous system.

The effect of exercise is not only chemic and mechanic, but also physiologic.

The voluntary movements are what distinguish animals from plants.

The higher we go in the scale of animal life, the more perfect is the mechanism for executing the various movements necessary to its existence. We find a finer muscular development in connection with a more highly developed *nervous system.*

Involuntary motions are adjusted by the *sympathetic nervous system*, while the voluntary movements are controlled and regulated by the *cerebro-spinal nervous system.*

That mysterious power which we call *will* imparts, at times, an impulse to muscular activity, and at others it restrains and impedes it.

Whatever the nature of the will, we know that when an impulse is generated in the brain it is carried to the nerves of the spinal cord, and from them to the peripheral nerves, and thence to the muscles, which causes what we call contraction.

Thus we see that exercise is not so simple a thing as is commonly supposed, *but, on the contrary, it is a complex process involving the brain, the spine, the nerves, and the muscles.*

As the activity of a muscle produces a constant change in the circulation, so this same action will greatly influence the *substance* of the nerves themselves.

This applies only to motor nerves, although some authors claim that exercise has an indirect effect upon the central nervous system.

At times physicians employ certain remedies called **derivatives,** the object of which is to relieve certain parts of the body. For instance, by the use of purgatives, to relieve portal congestion or to remove a sluggish circulation in the brain. In some mental disorders, as in melancholy or hysteria, the same theory directs that the mind should be constantly employed, so that the patient may have no time to think of himself.

Again, when there is a disturbance in the normal condition of the motor nerves, as in spasms, it may be removed by a strong and decided impression upon the central nervous system through sorrow, sudden terror, etc., or by an impression upon the nerves, by burning.

When there is any disturbance in the central nervous system, we can often, by employing agents to act upon the motor nerves, remove its cause.

We reach this conclusion because persons suffering from irritation of the central nervous system are generally those who use their motor nerves but little. Again, it is a common experience for the well-trained masseur to see these patients improve very rapidly, and be finally cured by fixed duplicated active movements.

Thus we conclude that active movements have a beneficial effect upon the nervous system, direct upon the motor nerves, and indirect, upon the central nerves.

What we have said about the effects of the movements has been of a general character, but it is necessary to understand the *local* effects upon the different organs of the body.

When treating a local affection, the movements or manipulations are to be applied in such a way that the affected part will derive the benefit. When the circulation is feeble in certain parts, the muscles in the neighborhood must be made to act, so that the blood will circulate more freely in the part diseased.

APPLICATION OF MASSAGE AND THE SWEDISH MOVEMENTS TO VARIOUS DISEASES OF THE BODY

The movement treatment, being an invigorating remedy, is recommended principally for chronic diseases where either the whole organism or only a part is weakened.

The prescriptions of massage and movements; given here are only mentioned in a general waye the operator must use them only after a careful consideration. What may be beneficial to one individual may injure another.

The operator should consequently use such movements and manipulations as he finds suitable to the individual case, in the meantime being guided by the prescriptions here mentioned.

It is necessary in all cases to note how the patient bears each movement. If any are too strong, they must be omitted, only to be resumed as the patient's strength increases.

During the first treatments great care should be taken not to overtax the patient's strength; *it is always better to do too little than too much*—the one is much easier remedied than the other.

GENERAL WEAKNESS

Apply general massage. Follow with passive flexions and extensions, rotations and pressings. Finally give percussion of the back, if the patient's strength permits.

The first treatments should last from twenty to thirty-five minutes, gradually increasing to an hour at the end of the first week. *Daily treatments are often necessary.*

Under this heading come most of the affections or rather conditions treated by general massage; for instance, when a patient is convalescent after fevers (typhoid, scarlatina), after operations, when the body is emaciated, in many conditions of nervous disorders, and in general when we propose the treatment as a tonic instead of outdoor exercise.

ANEMIA

For this disease some authors recommend general massage of the whole body, others recommend a complete series of movements. *A series of well selected movements in connection with the general massage* will perhaps be the most effective agent in renewing the blood. The treatment must be only by passive movements, and such as will aid the *digestion*, the *circulation* and the *respiration*.

When the patient is very feeble, use only the general massage, gradually commencing with the movements as the strength increases. All exercises should be passive, so as not to overtax the patient.

The following series, recommended by Professor Hartelius, of Stockholm, Sweden, has frequently been used with success:

1. S. rotation of the arms.[1]
2. Half L. rotation of feet.
3. Massage of abdomen.
4. S. rotation of arms.
5. S. rotation of body.
6. Half L. flexion and extension of legs.
7. St. percussion[2] of back.

The first movement is for respiration, extending the chest. The air is inspired more freely and a greater quantity of oxygen brought in contact with the blood. Eight to twelve times. The second carries the blood to the feet, which are generally cold; the third aids digestion and increases the appetite; the fourth, see 1; the fifth affects the great venous system; the sixth increases circulation in the lower extremities; the seventh has a refreshing action on the whole system.

The movements are scientifically arranged to remove the tired feeling, the loss of appetite, the cold hands and feet, the backache, and all symptoms we find in an anemic patient.

If there be any abdominal affections, special attention must be paid to them in the selection of the movements.

[1] S. means sitting; St., standing; L., lying; Kn., kneeling; Sp., suspending.

[2] Whenever the expression "percussion" is used, the author means hacking.

HYSTERIA

For hysteria we use such manipulations as will act directly upon the peripheric nervous system. The general massage, followed by a few rotary movements of the extremities, is to be recommended.

CHOREA

If the disease has advanced so far that the child has no control whatever over the limbs, place him on a couch or bed, one operator standing at the head, holding the arms, another standing at the feet, grasping the lower extremities. Begin with gentle stroking with the palm of the hand over the extremities and the chest, gradually increasing the strength; then turn the patient over on his face, and continue the firm stroking over the back and neck. The full treatment should last an hour, and be repeated daily four or five times. (Blaché.) As soon as improvement is visible, begin with certain passive movements, such as flexion and extension of the extremities, separating and closing of the knees, bending of the head, depression and elevation of the arms.

The patient is soon able to take duplicated active movements, and is finally instructed in general active movements or calisthenics, the operator keeping exact time.

Strong, persistent treatment every day, with special attention to the duplicated active movements, will yield good results.—Functional spasm often yields to persistent massage treatment whereas hysterical spasm offers more resistance.—[*Editor.*]

PLETHORA

In this affection we use movements such as will attract the blood from the head and produce muscular activity.

The most important part of our treatment is the massage of the neck and head. By the former we can relieve the blood-pressure on the brain to a remarkable extent, the patient often after the treatment telling us: "How much lighter my head feels." Both methods of massage of the neck may be used, but that of Hoeffinger should be selected as the introductory massage, to reach the deeper veins and give an outlet for the congested circulation.

1. Massage of neck and head.
2. Half L. rotation of leg.
3. S. rotation of body.
4. Half L. rotation of feet.
5. S. rotation of head.
6. Kn. turning of body.
7. Beating of sacrum.
8. S. rotation of arms.
9. S. percussion of head, with shaking and stroking.

INSOMNIA

There are certain movements which so affect the central or the sympathetic nerve-system that they are called by some authors "sleeping-movements."

As a rule, the general active movements are sufficient. The treatment should always be applied at bedtime. The following manipulations and treatments will prove beneficial:

1. Light general massage.
2. S. Depression and elevation of arms.
3. Half L. flexion and extension of legs.
4. S. turning of body.
5. Separating and closing of arms.
6. L. raising of body.
7. St. bending of knees.
8. Massage of neck and head.
9. Head clapping and stroking.

HEADACHES

During the past few years the author has had such exceptional results in the treatment of peripheral headaches that he wishes to pay some special attention to their treatment by massage. It has been clearly established that many cases of headaches with negative eye-conditions have been cured by thorough massage of the neck and head. Dr. Gustaf Norström has shown us in his excellent little book on headaches, that many of these cases are caused by myositic deposits in the neck, generally in the nape, but frequently also in the respective anatomical extremes of the neck. This may seem rather strange to many, but the trained masseur knows and almost daily experiences the fact that the "spontaneous pain has not always the same seat as the lesion."

The cases are readily defined; the oculist reports that there is no condition of the eyes that could possibly cause the suffering. Then let us carefully examine the neck and head. The first thing to look for is this: is there a cerebral congestion of some standing? Hoeffinger's method of massage of the neck will tell us that. We as a rule find this congestion, particularly in the plethorics who have obstructions to the circulation in the upper part of the trunk. In the nape of the neck we find many lumps or myositic deposits, which in contradistinction to the ganglia and lymphatic glands are movable only with the particular muscle of which they form a part. Pressing of a myositic deposit will cause acute pain, often extending to the supraorbital nerve and eyelid of the corresponding side. These deposits may be recognized in three stages or degrees (Norström): we may have a swelling only, or a resistive touch, or an actual induration where the consistency is very hard and the deposit consequently well defined.

Now to the practical application of masssage for headaches. First of all we must give strong, thorough strokings with both hands from the base of the skull to the acromion processes. This is our introductory massage to relieve not only the cerebral congestion, but also the pronounced congestion of the nape of the neck. The first few treatments should consist of these manipulations only, with a few strokings of the head added, but as soon as we can clearly define the deposits we commence with our strong frictions and kneadings, picking up the lump separately and squeezing it between the thumb and fingers. This causes pain often to such a degree that it becomes necessary to allow the patient some rest occasionally; the whole treatment should never exceed twenty minutes, and by that time not only the patient but also the operator has had enough! The patient should be compelled to take a rest in a recumbent position for fifteen minutes after the treatment.

It is not sufficient to massage the muscles and their deposits only but the nerves of the scalp and of the forehead should receive attention, particularly in those cases where we are able to find local structural changes.

In regard to the Swedish movements we have principally the following as the most useful:

1. Susp. bending of head (concentric).
2. Sitting bending of head.
3. St. bending of turned body sideways.
4. Sitting turning of the head.
5. Ostrom's combined resp. movement (see page 96).

In the movements marked 3 and 5 the reader will notice that the author wishes to act upon the organs of the trunk which are apt to become congested, especially the liver. I have had several cases of headaches in plethorics which did not yield at all until I carefully treated the liver.

It is well to mention that in all cases the author has watched and treated, there was invariably either a history of gout, rheumatism or a congested liver with distended gall-bladder. Consequently we must not lose sight of the necessity of proper diet and medication to prevent the further formation of deposits—massage is effective only for what has been formed by impaired digestion and stored up in the muscles by locally impaired circulation.

APOPLEXY

Experience shows that even old cases of paralysis are very often improved, and sometimes completely cured, by mechanotherapy. Its advantages consist in being able to work upon the entire nerve-system as soon as the least activity is apparent in the affected side.

The massage is used at first to stimulate the nerves and to increase nutrition. It will *always* be of some benefit, provided the system has power to react.

In treating a case of paralysis the operator should remember two special points:

1. Find out which muscles are affected and treat them and their nerve-supplies with massage.

2. Overcome the contraction of the antagonists by movements, or if necessary by braces.

Where there is active power in the affected side,

use, in connection with the massage, the following movements (for instance, for the right side):

1. S. rotation of arms.
2. Half L. rotation of legs.
3. S. rotation of right shoulder.
4. Flexion and extension of right leg.
5. Depression and elevation of right arm.
6. Pressing and shaking of right leg.
7. Pressing and shaking of right arm.
8. Percussion of back.

It is generally the best plan not to start the massage until three weeks after the stroke. The operator should always remember to select such manipulations and movements as will prevent a rush of blood to the cerebrum.

Paralysis from accident, gout or rheumatism, is very often treated by massage, the result depending upon the condition of the affected nerves. When caused by poison, mechanotherapy is recommended principally as a stimulating remedy, when the patient is convalescent. In paralysis from lead-poisoning massage is an excellent remedy.

The necessity of a knowledge of anatomy on the part of the operator is more apparent in treating cases of paralysis than any others. Careful attention should be paid to the facial muscles if *required*.

In a Swedish journal is recorded a case of an eighteen-year-old patient paralyzed in one leg from childhood. He was treated twice daily for three consecutive years by thorough massage and movements, and at the age of twenty-one his leg was restored to its natural size and strength.

It is astonishing what the inunction of cod-liver oil in connection with the massage will do in some cases of paralysis.—Recent experiments in the treatment of cerebral paralysis have advanced the theory, that by immobilization of corresponding unaffected muscles, the paralyzed ones quicker regain normal function.—[*Editor.*]

INFANTILE PARALYSIS

In this obscure and troublesome affection scientific massage has won some of its greatest victories. With the aid of the electric current we first find out which muscles or which groups of muscles are affected. This should not be done however until one full month from the day of the first attack. It is a well acknowledged fact that the amount of damage done to the tissues will all depend upon how soon the disease is properly recognized, so as to promptly apply the counter irritation to both sides of the whole spinal column.

When we begin the massage we should give *strokings* only over the whole affected limb to increase nutrition and tone up the different parts, but the deep massage should at first be given *only* to the most affected muscles and their nerve supply, the other or stronger groups being severely let alone. In my own practice I have often taken cases of this trouble and in a short time gotten the most marked improvement simply by adhering to the above rule, when before the ordinary "rubbing-massage" had been tried for a year or more and failed to give any result. It seems to me that the attending physician should plainly write out his prescription or the massage to be faithfully filled by a competent operator.

We stretch the spinal column by movements or better still by suspension as the patient gains strength and I always arrange a horizontal bar with cleats in a doorway so that I have two heights, one for the child sitting and one for the standing position. When the braces are first put on I use a double bar fitting the height of the child like a crutch; there is also another cross-bar below to put the hands on; the uprights are slanting inward and only room enough is given for the child to get through. This is an excellent arrangement in the early starting of teaching coordination. My next move is generally to let the child push the rolling chair, if old enough; by this time there is more coordination, he will begin to balance at first for a minute, then more and more every day; now we may begin with crutches cut rather short so as to get a slight forward bend which helps to steady the patient in balancing; then only one crutch and a cane and finally the one cane. Of course it will be understood that in the meantime the child has medical tonic treatment also electricity and hydrotherapy in connection with the massage. The treatment must be given every day if there is to be any result expected.

A careful record should be kept and the most accurate measurements taken at fixed intervals. The salt air at the seashore for a short interval seems to have a wonderfully beneficial effect upon these cases and it is well to stop the massage occasionally for a week or so for a trip to the shore. The improvement will afterward be so much more rapid.

The movements which I use are principally for the spine as Lying raising of the body. At first it is often necessary to tie a sheet around the footboard of the bed and have the patient try to pull himself up or it may be necessary for the operator or the mother who should be taught how to give these movements, to assist the child by placing the hand between the shoulder blades. Suspension, passive and active we have already discussed. Now in regard to the movements for the extremities used in connection with our massage we will take a fairly typical leg for demonstration: the foot is constantly extended, hence we flex the foot (much easier done if the leg is flexed at the same time) to overcome the contraction of the extensors. The foot is not only extended but also everted; consequently we invert it with our flexion. The same child can draw her leg up but can not possibly push it down or in any way extend it, hence we practise extension of the leg; the right leg she can bring in to the median line hence her adductors of the right side are saved, but she lacks power of rotation outward so we give that movement to act upon the biceps femoris and the gluteus maximus. The operator must of necessity study out each individual case to obtain good result, as there are never two cases of poliomyelitis exactly alike.

On account of the excellent results that the author has had in treating this affection, it has frequently been suggested that he had some new, secret methods of treatment, but such is not the case and any intelligent and qualified operator will by following the above instructions have the same good results. It should also be mentioned that I frequently make use of exercises similar to those described by Fraenkel to help along coordination. On a board I draw two large, round points connected with a line and make the child learn to follow this; afterwards I make a triangle in the same way and later a semi-circle or an ellipse. I have found these simple exercises of great practical value.

TABES

Apply massage of the back in connection with pressing. Massage of the abdomen, with pressing above the bladder and pressing and shaking of the extremities, are frequently used. Some authors recommend extension of the legs, pulling of the legs and beating of the sacrum. The movements should be refreshing and invigorating and great care should be taken not to overexert the patient.

A rest in bed for six weeks with intelligently applied massage and inunctions, if indicated, have

9

given the most satisfactory results in the author's experience, including some sixty cases.

Of all movements recommended by the authors on mechanotherapeutics in the treatment of locomotor ataxia none *equals* the pulling of the legs. Place the patient perfectly flat on his back without head-rest; grasp with one hand around the ankle, with the other firmly above the knee—pulling downward slowly without jerking. Carefully and properly applied, this simple movement will often relieve the most agonizing ataxic pains.

As trained nurses are often requested by the attending physician to inunct a patient with blue ointment in this affection, and as the author has seen several cases in which the "inunction" consisted of merely placing the prescribed quantity in the groin or axilla, he considers it proper to here give the correct method of inunction as recommended by Dr. Sigmund. The patient should, if possible, take a hot bath as a preparation. If that, for some reason, be impossible, it becomes the operator's duty to wash the part inuncted, either with soap and warm water or with alcohol and water, to dissolve the fat in the pores. The ointment should be worked in with moderate friction by the palm of the hand: on the first day on the inside of the legs; on the second day on the outside of the thighs; on the third day on the sides of the trunk; on the fourth day on the back; on the fifth day on the inside of the arms; on the sixth day commence a new series. In twenty to thirty minutes the seance is completed. The operator should wear a glove to protect himself from absorbing the drug. In the friction it is best to try to describe a figure eight, unless the parts are heavily covered with hair—then work in a circle. If the patient desires to conceal the fact that he is taking the inunction, wash the parts worked upon and remove every trace of the proceeding. The best result will be accomplished if the drug is allowed to remain on the skin to be gradually absorbed. Three hot baths a week are generally recommended.

The new preparation "Mercury-Vasogen" is now generally used for inunction and it is far superior to the blue ointment as it works in so much quicker and does not leave a disagreeable odor. Besides it has been the author's experience that it does not produce any skin-affections, while the blue ointment is very apt to cause not only local irritations of the parts inuncted, but also eczema and erythema.

NEURALGIA

Diseases of the peripheric nerves are more successfully treated by mechanotherapy than are affections of the central nerve-system. Most neuralgias yield readily to massage, and in cases of *sciatica* it has been used with most excellent results.

For the latter disease, if the right leg is affected, use:

1. Stroking of right leg (from behind).

2. Percussion and beating over the nerve.
3. Flexion and extension of right leg.
4. Raising of leg.
5. Beating of sacrum and right leg.

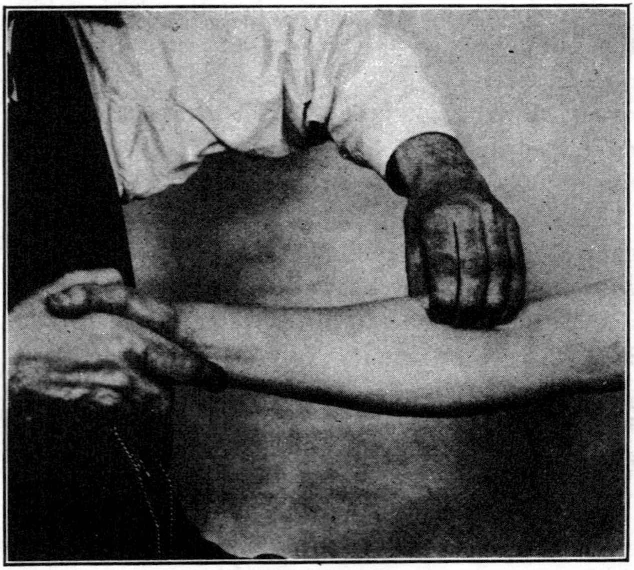

FIG. 110.—Right Method of Stroking Radial Nerve Supporting Below.

Some of the manipulations must be repeated in the series five or six times. In raising the leg, place it, if necessary, on the shoulder, and, bending up and down, stretch the sciatic nerve as much as possible.

Rheumatic neuralgia in other nerves, as in the

trigeminus, so often found in anemic women, is often relieved by massage in a few treatments.

Use freely punctation over superficial nerves, and firm kneading and stroking with the thumbs. If the nerve is very tender, begin with a slight introductory stroking with the thumb.

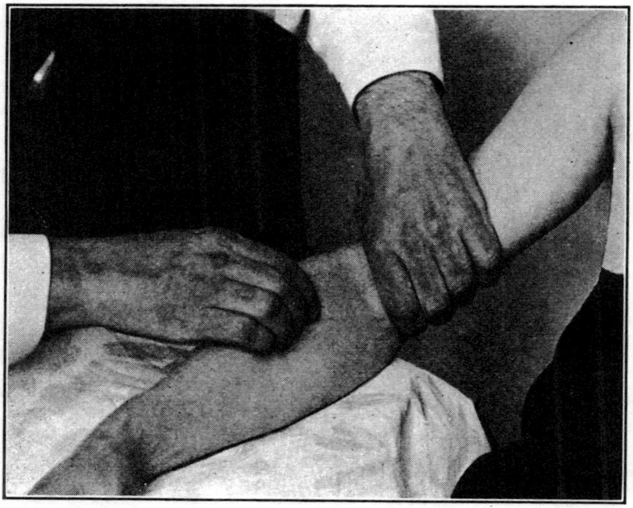

FIG. 111.—Wrong Method of Stroking. Note Left Hand Supporting Above Part Manipulated.

In some cases it may be advisable to use massage of the head, as described in Local Massage.

Massage of the neck (Hoeffinger's method) is an excellent remedy for many forms of neuralgia of the head and face.

NEURITIS

Neuritis is an inflammation of the nerve-trunks with pain, specially intensified by pressure. Gentle massage in the form of strokings is indicated from the beginning. In a case of neuritis of the arm we treat the brachial plexus carefully and stroke gently up-

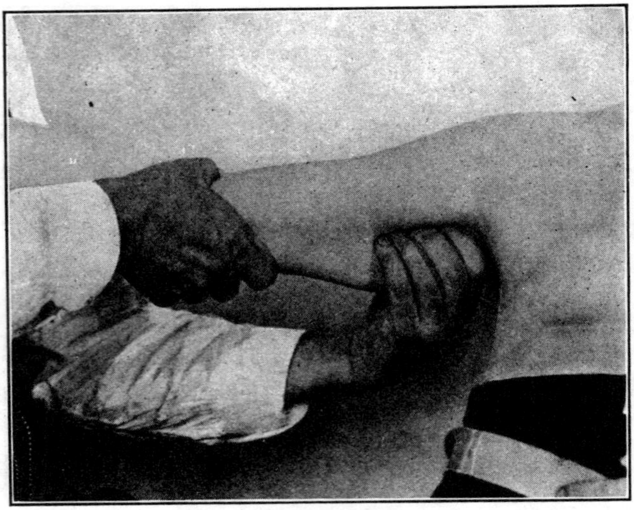

FIG. 112.—Stroking of the Brachial Nerves.

ward from the finger-tips to the spinal column. It is best to have the arm well supported in a sling broad enough to fully support the whole length of the forearm.

In multiple neuritis we have had most excellent results from massage gently applied. It will not do to treat a neuritis—no matter of what cause—with deep pressure as the nerves are extremely tender and the inflammation will be increased. The strokings help because they relieve the blood tension along the nerve-tract. If the operator only remembers this rule of care, we shall not hear any more complaints that massage is not indicated in the treatment of neuritis.

The author favored the use of "Eucalyptus liniment" from which he claimed good results. Rub the affected part with

Oil of Eucalyptus.................. 1 oz.
Camphor Petrogen (Wyeth)........ 2 oz.

[*Editor*]

PROGRESSIVE MUSCULAR ATROPHY

Use massage in the neighborhood of the affected muscles and upon them, and such movements as are calculated to increase circulation through the diseased parts.

Suppose a case of atrophy in the deltoid and supraspinatus; the following treatment should be used:

1. Massage of the arm from the fingers up to the trapezius.
2. Rotation of the hand.
3. Flexion and extension of the arm.
4. Rotation of the shoulder.

5. Firm hacking or clapping upon the whole arm, and especially around the shoulder.

6. Vibrations over brachial plexus.

WRITERS' CRAMP

Use massage from the tips of the fingers to the shoulder. Rotation, turning, flexion, and extension of the hand and arm may be used as the patient grows stronger, but massage is the principal part of the treatment.

The operator must be careful not to overtax his patient's strength. In beginning only treat the hand and forearm from ten to fifteen minutes. —The prognosis in trade neurosis is not particularly good, but I think it is most generally accepted, that massage and movements are the most effective means, and should at least be given a fair trial.—[*Editor.*]

SPLANCHNIC NEURASTHENIA

So important has this functional disturbance lately become in this country that it is high time that its proper mechanical treatment be analyzed. As Dr. Abrams so clearly puts it, the principal symptoms are: "Abdominal sensitiveness, tenderness of the liver and enlargement of that organ and gaseous accumulation in the bowels."

In regard to the treatment we have to remember that physiologists have proven to us the fact that the abdominal veins are very elastic and that they are really capable of holding at one time the total blood volume of the whole body. In splanchnic neurasthenia we have first of all to overcome the intense *congestion* of blood in the splanchnic and abdominal veins in general.

We begin with massage of the liver, so as to give the venous circulation a free outlet. The patient is lying on his left side with the right arm over his head and the operator carefully works over the whole hepatic region not forgetting the three splanchnic nerves. Many "paths and—practics" would have you believe that they are the only ones who pay proper attention to organic nerve-supply, but it is not true. Fortunately we possess the plain writing of P. H. Ling and his true pupils published almost one hundred years ago to conclusively prove that the Swedish mechanical operator, or medical gymnast who is properly trained always is taught to attend to the nerve-supply of the individual organ or muscle that he may be treating. The massage of the abdomen in general is now given so as to improve the muscular tone and overcome the local congestion. Massage of the neck is also given.

As we gain ground we instruct the patient in some of those Swedish movements which compress the viscera and tone up the whole abdomen. Other therapeutics in the shape of electricity and hot-cold sponge baths are most effective, and the reader who is specially interested in the rational treatment of the affection, should procure that excellent work: "The Blues" by Dr. Albert Abrams.

AFFECTIONS OF THE RESPIRATORY ORGANS

Respiration is altogether mechanical, depending upon the constitution of the muscles of the chest, the extension of the latter, and the quantity of air inspired. If the capacity of the lungs be increased, all difficulty of breathing, coughs, etc., caused by an imperfect respiration, will soon disappear.

In cases where defective respiration is the result of weakness of the respiratory muscles or of deformities of the chest, the movements have proved the best means for increasing the capacity of the respiratory organs (see page 96).

The effect of the medical gymnastics is to necessitate frequent and deep inspirations, and more complete expiration, thus increasing the capacity of the lungs, promoting pulmonary circulation and causing an increased oxygenation of the venous blood.

CATARRH OF THE LUNGS

Certain manipulations (hacking, clapping and shaking) on the chest have been used to induce expectoration. The movements must be such as to cause muscular activity and increase the secretion from the skin. Action upon the digestive organs will produce a derivative effect upon the lungs.

PHARYNGITIS AND LARYNGITIS

Because massage of the neck and throat induces such an evacuation of the blood-vessels, it has been freely used for acute catarrh of the pharynx, trachea and nose. We are able by careful examination of the inflamed mucous membranes, before and after the application of massage, to notice directly the result. Not the local symptoms only, but the headache, the pain in the forehead, the dizziness, etc., resulting from the stagnation of blood, disappear after a few treatments. By massage we also act upon the tonsils and other glands, thus assisting expectoration.

Croup may sometimes be speedily relieved. *Weiss* has noted a case of croup in which a single application removed the most imminent peril.

The massage of the neck and throat ought to be more freely used for these affections.

CONSUMPTION

Some respiratory movements are used to make the patient more comfortable, increasing the inspiration and assisting the heart in its action.

Massage of the lower extremities is sometimes applied to relieve the swelling and to increase the circulation.

General massage is often recommended as a tonic, but should always be given in the forenoon, and never at night, as it has then a decided tendency to increase the night sweats.

BRONCHITIS, NERVOUS ASTHMA, ETC.,

are frequently treated by massage, generally in the form of strokings of the entire chest, the patient inspiring deeply at the same time. The séance must not exceed twenty minutes.

COLDS

So many persons suffer with recurrent colds in our changeable climate that we deem it well to pay some attention to the matter. A cold is an inflammation of the mucous membrane lining the upper respiratory passages. One region is generally more affected than the others. A cold begins with a congestion and its principal causes are: (1) "chilling the skin in a person whose skin is sensitive and tender to the changes of temperature, causing a contraction of the superficial blood-vessels, and driving an excess of blood to the deeper structures of the body; (2) local irritation to an already congested respiratory tract, by the inhalation of polluted air, and air containing irritating substances such as dust, smoke, gases, etc."

Colds are most common in winter time, not on account of the cold weather but because at that time we breathe the most impure air, everything often being shut up in order to keep warm.

To prevent colds we must consequently breathe pure air and keep the function of the skin normal. This latter is best accomplished by proper *daily* bathing, massage and exercise. For the younger person we think nothing better than a cool sponge off with brisk friction every morning in a room of a temperature never less than 70° F. For older persons and for those not so very robust we recommend the hot-cold spray bath. The person sits in a tub with warm water up to the hips; now spray the spine, neck and chest with cool water, starting with a temperature of 85° F., and gradually in the course of a week or two, lowering it down to 50° F. Half a minute is enough at first. A strong self-massage with a rough rubber sponge or wash cloth is advisable, but the patient should always rub himself perfectly dry with a rough towel. If weak this must of course be done by an attendant.

If the patient has the opportunity of scientific massage for half an hour each morning so much the better; if not we must teach him some few effective movements to be practised every morning after his bath. The following are good:

1. Standing rotation of arms.
2. Ostrom's combined resp. movement.
3. St. bending of the body forward and backward.
4. Deep knee bend.
5. St. bending of the body sideways.

We do not wish the reader to lose sight of the fact that there are certain remedies which, if taken in the very incipiency of a cold, are really specific in their effect.

DISEASES OF THE HEART

Massage and movements are indicated in affections of the heart caused by nervous debility, anemia, diseases of the stomach, etc. The movements mostly used are:

Sitting, raising of the chest, with shaking, to produce strong respiration;

Rotation of the extremities, to assist the heart in its action;

Rotation and turning of the body, to give effect upon the great venous system;

Centripetal stroking, to remove the subcutaneous effusions.

In organic diseases of the heart, movements are recommended by some of the most eminent physicians. They apply movements to support the heart in its action, generally using such as will increase the circulation in the distant parts of the body.

Within the last few years a new system of exercise for heart-affections has been developed by Dr. August Schott, of Bad Nauheim, Germany. The results have at times been remarkable. He employs the effervescent Nauheim water, as a rule daily, and directs a series of resistive exercises (original Swedish movements) to be given daily, or every other day if the patient is too weak. The general massage—gently applied—is too often lost sight of as a most excellent preparation for this particular movement cure. All the movements are duplicated-active, and the resistance should be so applied as not to interfere with the circulation—preferably, when possible, with the palmar surface of the hand. Every movement should be performed slowly, and the operator should watch his patient most carefully. At first the séance should last but ten minutes, to be gradually and carefully increased to thirty minutes. A rest should be allowed after each movement, and no exercise is to be applied more than once in each series. The operator should carefully guard against the following symptoms:

1. Intermission of the pulse.
2. Weakness of the pulse.
3. Increased respiration.
4. Palpitation of the heart.
5. Dilatation of the nostrils.
6. General feeling of discomfort.

When any of the above-mentioned symptoms appear allow a few minutes' rest; or, if necessary, stop the treatment for the day. It is customary to take the pulse and respiration before starting, during the middle of the séance, and at its close. A careful record should be kept for the reference of the attending physician.

The **principal Schott exercises** are:

1. Separating and closing of arms.
2. Flexion and extension of arms.
3. Raising of the arms upward.
4. Rotation of the arms.
5. Pronation and supination of the forearm.

6. Flexion and extension of the hand.
7. Flexion and extension of the fingers.
8. Abduction and adduction of the fingers.
9. St. bending of the body forward and backward.
10. S. bending of the body sideways.
11. S. rotation of the body.
12. Same as 1, with clenched fist.
13. Same as 2, with clenched fist.
14. St. arms extended forward and backward.
15. L. flexion and extension of the leg.
16. L. flexion and extension of the foot.
17. L. separation and closing of the thighs or legs.
18. St. leg extended forward and backward.

Careful operators are sometimes requested to apply treatment locally; then use massage of the chest, as previously described, with hacking in small circles over the cardiac region. Palmar vibrations are also used. In the European institutes of medical gymnastics it is quite common to see the vibrations applied over the heart. The operator then places his arm upon the artificial vibrator and the wave-like movements are transferred to the cardiac region through the semi-flexed and abducted fingers. Except when especially requested by a physician, however, this local application is seldom used. Gentle respiratory movements should always form the conclusion of the treatment, and an hour's rest should be rigidly insisted upon.

DISEASES OF THE DIGESTIVE ORGANS

In applying mechanotherapy for these affections, we must call attention to the fact that most of them develop from circulatory disturbances, the vessels being relaxed.

There are different ways to apply massage of the stomach; one has already been described. Another way is to place the fingers about two inches below the ribs and, with pressing, move the hand upward in connection with shaking. In a special position (half lying, with the knees flexed, so as to relax the abdominal muscles, crook-half-lying) it is quite easy to reach the stomach by pressing, shaking and kneading.

Massage of the stomach is indicated in all affections caused by circulatory disturbances or general weakness (atony) of the parts.

DYSPEPSIA

1. Massage of the stomach and the abdomen (fifteen minutes).
2. Percussion of the back.
3. High St. pulling of legs.
4. S. turning of body.
5. Flexion and extension of legs.
6. S. rotation of arms.

The movements are repeated.

HABITUAL CONSTIPATION

Massage and movements are now freely used for constipation. The treatment must always be local in the beginning, and afterward constitutional.

1. Local massage (ten to twenty minutes).
2. St. bending of knees (hands on hips).
3. L. raising body.
4. S. turning of body.

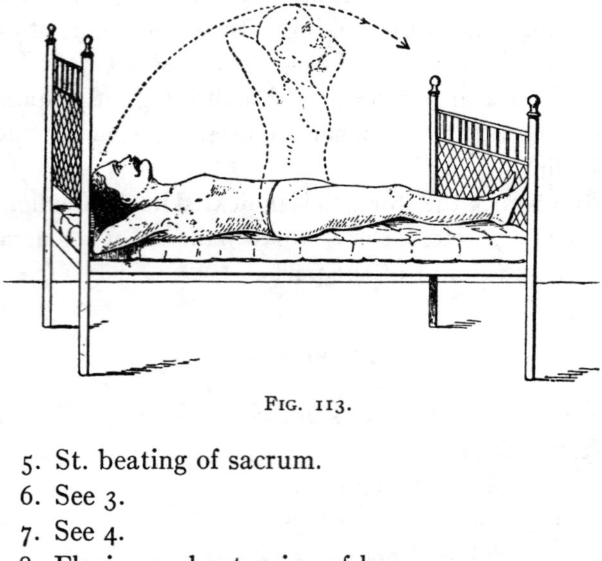

FIG. 113.

5. St. beating of sacrum.
6. See 3.
7. See 4.
8. Flexion and extension of legs.
9. St. percussion of back.

Schreiber says: "Chronic constipation offers the most signal success to mechanotherapy, for it is possible to make direct mechanical pressure upon the celiac and hypogastric plexuses, and through these to reflexly excite peristalsis; furthermore, the vasomotor nerves and the intestinal muscular fibers are directly stimulated by the squeezing to which they can be subjected." The treatment is indeed very effective, and it is not rare to obtain an evacuation of the bowels immediately after the manipulations.

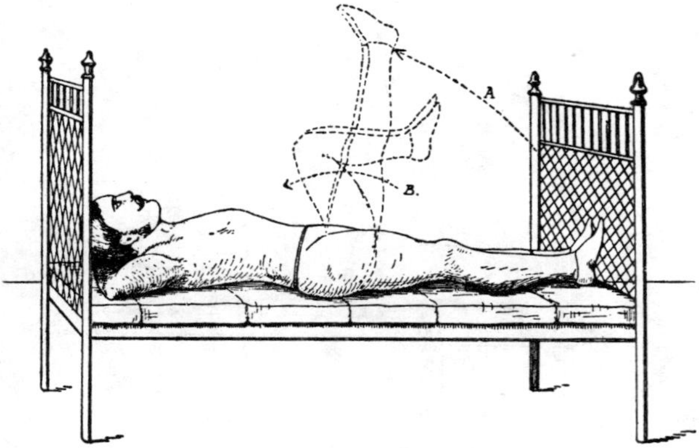

FIG. 114.

After the patient has taken a course of treatment he should be instructed to take every morning a few exercises to keep the bowels working properly. The patient will, as a rule, offer the common excuse he has no time for such a procedure, but the operator should rigidly insist upon it, telling him that he, by neglecting to take the exercises, may gradually lose the benefit of the course of treatment he has undergone, and incidentally, he may suggest to his patient simply to rise ten minutes earlier and he will have ample time to perform the movements. We have selected five of the most effective exercises easily performed in the bedroom.

As in Fig. 113, the patient should lie flat on his back, without head-rest, with hands clasped back of the head; he should slowly rise to a sitting position,

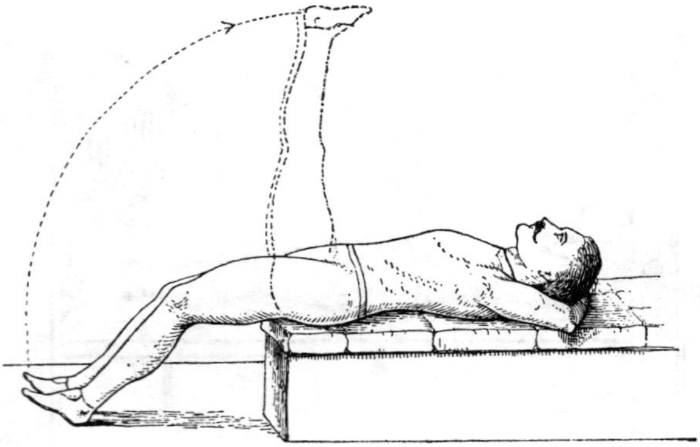

FIG. 115.

and, if able, even bend forward as much as possible. When first taking the movement he will have some difficulty in keeping his feet down; tell him to put a pillow or quilt on top of his feet. By this exercise we strongly compress the abdomen, aiding in fecal movement mechanically, increasing the general peristaltic action, and accelerating the secretions from the various glands. The following four exercises (see Figs. 114–117) are very similar in their effect, and they are so clearly illustrated that we do not deem it necessary to separately describe them. (The standing bending of the body should be carefully done by patients suffering from hemorrhoids.)

Constipation is of most frequent occurrence in infancy. Less than three evacuations a day indicate a constipated condition. Place the child flat on its back in the bed, or, if convenient, on the

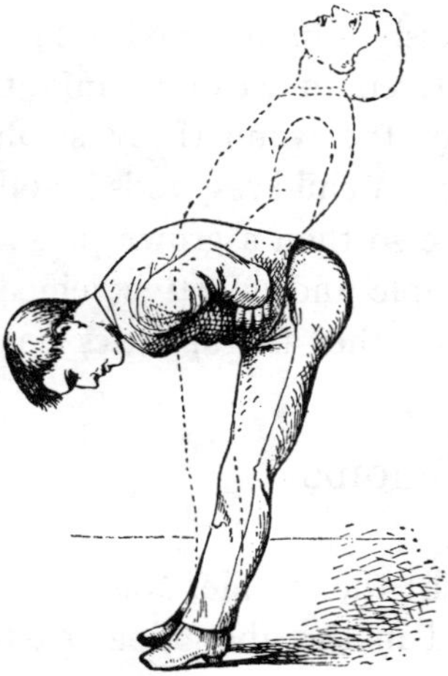

FIG. 116.

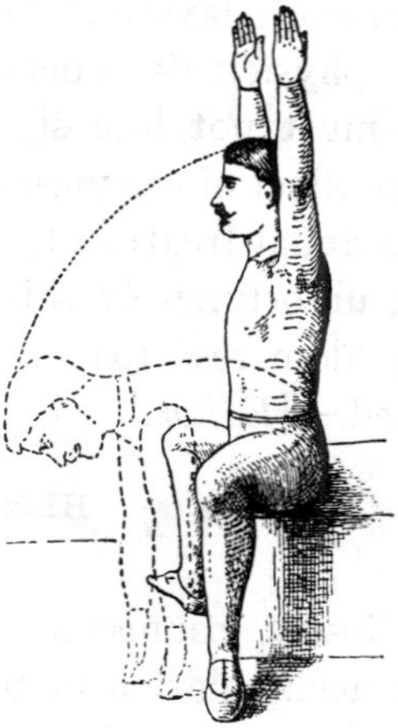

FIG. 117.

mother's lap; smear the abdominal wall with pure olive oil, and proceed with the massage of the abdomen as previously described, paying special attention to the various parts of the colon. Colic, so frequently caused by improper action of the bowels, is often quickly relieved by massage. If the abdomen is much distended, care and judgment must be used so that too much pressure is not applied. Pass lightly over the region of the transverse colon, and *never* use so much pressure on any part as to cause pain. Any intelligent mother can be properly instructed to treat her child for constipation, and such knowledge will often be very useful not only directly at the time, but also indirectly afterward, as it will often save the child from irritating and weakening laxatives carelessly administered without the physician's orders. Even in cases of infants, we must not lose sight of the wonderfully strong *tonic* effect of the massage.—A child responds readily to manual treatment; more so than a grown person, but unfortunately this simple and effective remedy is seldom resorted to until other therapeutics have failed.—[*Editor*.]

HEMORRHOIDS

Closely connected with the former disease is the accumulation of blood in the abdominal parts, called hemorrhoids.

By the manipulations on the abdomen we assist the intestines in their action; by rotation and turning of the body we control the great venous system, and by beating over the sacral region we increase the circulation in the region of the rectum relieving congestion in the Hemorrhoidal vein.

The following movements have been used with success:

1. Massage of the liver and the abdomen (ten to fifteen minutes). See page 21.
2. St. bending of knees.
3. Separating and closing of knees.
4. L. raising of body.
5. Rotation of legs.
6. Beating of sacrum.
7. Rotation and turning of body.

Although we highly recommend the movements for this affection, we must acknowledge that one treatment a day is not enough. The patient must be instructed in certain calisthenics which give a direct effect upon the great venous system.

OBESITY

Massage and Swedish movements have been used with great success in cases of obesity. Muscular exercise decreases the fat by promoting a more perfect oxygenation through the whole organism.

In connection with *firm* massage use the following movements:

1. Separating and closing of arms.
2. Separating and closing of legs.
3. L. raising of body.
4. St. bending of knees.
5. St. rotation of arms (active).
6. St. turning of body.

During the first treatments use only a few movements, gradually getting the patient used to them.

As pathologic changes in the texture of the blood-vessels are rather common in cases of obesity the operator should use careful judgment in regard to the strength of the manipulations.

Without proper diet massage will accomplish but very little.

Frequently the masseur will be asked by the patient how he can consistently claim that massage will reduce fat, and also in a thin person produce fat. When we desire to reduce fat we give firm massage, especially kneading, which produces heat; this causes combustion of fat. When we apply the treatment with the object of increasing weight we do so by building up the whole system and particularly the digestive organs. Whatever our aim may be, one of the most important parts of the treatment consists in teaching the patients how to breathe properly.

ENLARGEMENT OF THE LIVER

We use movements, that are calculated to increase the circulation through the great venous system.

1. S. rotation of arms.
2. L. rotation of feet.
3. S. raising of body.
4. L rotation of legs.
5. S. rotation of body.
6. St. flexion and extension of feet.
7. Massage of the liver with clapping.
8. Separating and closing of knees.

9. Vibrations over the liver.
10. St. percussion of back.

The movements must be performed twice a day, and the patient instructed in certain calisthenics.

DIABETES

Some authors report cases of diabetes successfully treated by mechanotherapy. Schreiber says: "The best effects will ensue when the greatest number of muscles are brought into play. It is necessary to select such movements as will call into action equally all the great muscle-groups."

In Paris, where diabetes is common, the patients are advised to take very strong bodily exercise. The quantity of sugar secreted must indicate a deficient oxygenation of the materials produced by the liver. Strong bodily exercise, which increases oxygenation in all the membranes of the body, ought to eliminate the abnormal presence of sugar.

The proper exercise for this affection is not yet well determined. When the patient has a constitution strong enough to bear the treatment, use the following movements:

1. St. percussion of back.
2. L. rotation of feet.
3. Separating and closing of arms.
4. S. bending of body backward.
5. Flexion and extension of legs.
6. Raising of body.

7. Flexion and extension of arms.
8. Separating and closing of knees.
9. Percussion of back.—Strong vibrations of the region of the pancreas stimulates that gland to increased secretion, the function of which is to transform sugar into glycogen.

UTERINE AFFECTIONS

Massage is applied directly to force the organs to contract, and the movements to regulate the circulation through the abdomen. Atony and dislocations of the organ are generally treated by massage; disturbances in regard to menstruation, only by movements.

AMENORRHEA

1. S. rotation of arms.
2. Rotation of feet.
3. S. turning of body (inspiration).
4. S. rotation of body.
5. Beating of sacrum.
6. Vibrations.
7. Rotation of arms.
8. St. percussion of back.

Some of the movements must be repeated several times in the series, but when treating extremely anemic women great care should be taken not to give too many.

DYSMENORRHEA

A great number of women suffer severe pain before and during the periods. In many of these cases we can by overcoming the local congestion give the greatest relief. We recommend:

1. Massage of the liver.
2. Massage of the whole abdomen.
3. St. rotation of arms.
4. L. rotation of feet.
5. St. rotation of body.
6. L. rotation of leg.
7. St. bending of turned body.
8. L. rotation of pelvis.

This treatment should be given to the patient at least two weeks before the period is expected, and she should be properly instructed how to take a few good movements to prevent the congestion of blood in the abdomen.

I have made the observation that women who lace tightly are always the greatest sufferers from dysmenorrhea.

AFFECTIONS OF THE BLADDER

We have here to deal with two common conditions: the retention of the urine and the incontinence of the urine. Both have been successfully treated by massage. Before starting the treatment the bladder should be emptied naturally, or artificially, if necessary.

Massage the whole abdomen first and then use strokings, frictions and vibrations (see page 57) locally.

In many nervous women especially at the climacteric period we find the symptom of frequent desire to urinate.

In such cases massage is an excellent remedy, vibrations being especially effective.

The bladder should never be treated mechanically except on the order of a physician, as there are many conditions in which massage may do a great deal of harm instead of good.

RHEUMATISM

The active movements, as well as pétrissage, hacking and beating of the affected parts, are of great benefit in cases of rheumatism. In severe attacks the treatment should be applied twice daily. The patient must move his limbs freely instead of keeping them inactive.

Begin with general massage around and over the affected part; continue with local massage on the diseased muscle or joint and finish the treatment with a few movements that give effect upon the circulation and respiration.

The operator should study his case carefully and by passive and active movements of the affected part try to localize the rheumatic deposits. How important this is will be clearly illustrated to the reader in the following case:

A gentlemen was sent to me for massage for a "rheumatic shoulder;" he had been treated for some time with massage applied locally, *i.e.*, right over and close to the joint. The result had been unsatisfactory and he had no faith in the treatment. The joint was carefully examined and was found all right. He could raise the arm and he could rotate it without pain or difficulty, but when I told him to throw the arm downward and backward, I then saw that his trouble was located in the latissimus dorsi. This muscle was then carefully treated and with very satisfactory result. He at first ridiculed the idea of curing an affected shoulder by treating the lower part of the back, but is today a very enthusiastic believer in scientific massage.

LUMBAGO

The patient should lie on his stomach with the abdomen supported by pillows. The operator should perform *firm* strokings with both hands over the lumbar region, from the spinal column toward the sides. In many cases it is well to give massage to the whole back and the glutei, as previously described.

The treatment must be given twice or three times daily. It generally takes from two to five days to conquer the trouble.

The following additional movements may be used:

1. St. bending of body.
2. L. raising of body.
3. S. bending of trunk.
4. S. raising of body.
5. Local vibration.

STIFF NECK

This affection is somewhat similar to lumbago and has been treated with like success. Begin with massage over the sterno-cleidomastoid and continue with pressing and shaking. A few (in the beginning passive) movements will finish the treatment. Though at first painful, the patient will in a few days be relieved by the treatment:

The following movements may be used:

1. S. or susp. bending of head.
2. S. turning of head.
3. S. rotation of head.

GOUT

Between the attacks massage is often prescribed, especially for *podagra.* The treatment must be given for general activity of the muscles.

1. St. bending of knees.
2. St. bending backward (back supported).
3. L. flexion and extension of legs.
4. S. turning of body.
5. S. rotation of arms.
6. Flexion and extension of feet.

7. S. raising of body.
8. Beating of sacrum.
9. Massage of stomach.
10. St. percussion of back.

The general massage is always of benefit and firm friction on the sole of the foot is very effective in cases of podagra.

Massage is of great value as a preventative of gout, as it eliminates urates and improves the general condition.—[*Editor*.]

LATERAL CURVATURE OF THE SPINE

There are few affections in which the movement treatment has met with more signal success than in this. The aim should be to invigorate and develop the weakened and pathologically changed muscles of the convex side so as to restore the natural equilibrium of the two sides. There are but four known and acknowledged methods of developing muscles locally—viz., massage, movements, electricity and hydropathy. As the two latter do not come within the province of this manual we shall only describe the two first mentioned.

The main things to remember in treating lateral curvature of the spine are:

1. To elongate the spine by suspension.
2. To raise the lower shoulder.
3. To counteract rotation of the vertebrae.
4. Massage to stimulate the muscles.

5. Selected movements in carefully selected positions.

Massage of the back is very useful in most all cases of scoliosis, and the operator should pay special attention to the convex side, particularly in the early stages of the affection. The treatment should be applied also to the glutei—the gluteus maximus in particular. Pinching is a very valuable manipulation, and when the patient becomes used to the massage apply it firmly, so as to reach the deeper layers of muscles. In older cases, it sometimes becomes necessary to treat also the muscles of the concave side, which from disuse have become atrophied. When the primary curve is high up, the cervical region should be faithfully attended to. Patient will often complain if too much pressure is used over the extreme convexity of the compensation curve—"the abrupt lower bend," as some patients style it.

We give here a list of the various Swedish movements used in the treatment of lateral curvature, and the operator who has been properly trained will experience no difficulty in selecting those which will prove the most beneficial to the individual case in question.

1. **St. Bending to the (Convex) Side.**—The patient stands with hands clasped on the back of the head. The operator places one hand on the highest point of the curvature and the other on the opposite hip, the patient bending slowly about ten

times. It may also be used as a single active movement.

2. **St. Bending to the (Convex) Side.**—Same movement as 1, only the patient places the arm

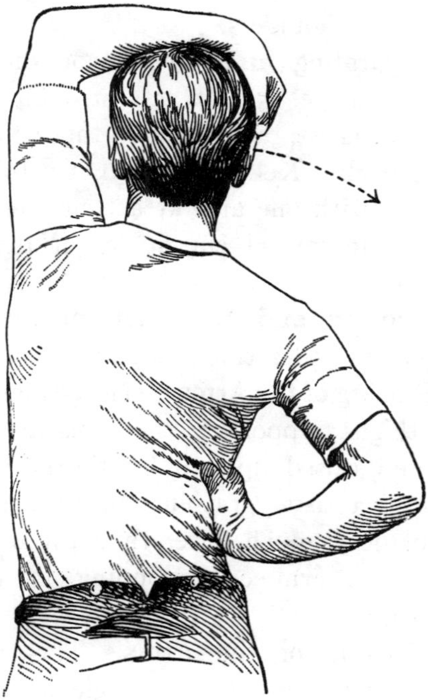

FIG. 118.

corresponding to the lower shoulder-blade over his head as demonstrated in Fig. 118, the other hand on hip. Single active or duplicated active, in the latter case the operator placing his hands as in 1.

3. **St. Rotation of the Arms.**—The patient should stand as erect as possible with arms at sides; he should carry his arms slowly forward and upward, then backward and downward. A very useful respiratory exercise, besides acting strongly upon the muscles of the shoulders.

4. **S. Separating and Closing of the Arms.**—Described on page 85. It acts strongly upon the muscles of the chest, but also upon those of the upper part of the back. Kellgren says that if this exercise is performed with one arm at a time, correction of the rotation in lateral curvatures of the spine is produced.

5. **St. Flexion and Extension of the Arms.**—This movement is described on page 82.

6. **St. Raising of the Arms.**—The patient is standing with thighs supported; the arms are extended outward and raised upward by the patient, while the operator resists, grasping the wrists. If one shoulder-blade is much lower than the other, work only with the arm corresponding to the lower shoulder-blade.

7. **St. Raising of the Arms.**—This movement is the same as No. 6, only it is single active; that is, the patient performs it himself. He should raise his arms from the sides to above his head with a deep inhalation, afterward lower them slowly to original position, and exhale while doing so.

8. **St. Bending of the Body Forward and Backward.**—(See Fig. 82.) The patient should place his

hands on his hips or clasp them on the back of his head. Another form of this exercise is performed in the following way: The patient stands with his limbs separated and his arms stretched straight up; he should bend slowly forward until the tips of the fingers touch the floor (see Fig. 83).

9. **L. Extension of the Back.**—The patient is lying with legs on couch, the trunk extending; the operator supports the feet; the patient bends his body upward as far as possible. This is a very effective movement and must be given with care. At first it is safest to have some one to aid in holding the patient. He may place his hands on his hips, or clasp them on the back of the head; after he grows stronger he may keep them extended straight forward parallel with the ears.

10. **L. on the Side, Bending the Trunk.**—The patient is lying with legs on couch and trunk extended in side position, the *convex side up* and the feet supported. The bending should be performed slowly.

11. **S. Raising of the Body.**—The patient sitting on a stool or a turned chair with hands on back of head, bends forward, the operator resisting him when he resumes the original position. The lower shoulder may be raised up, as the operator has perfect control of the trunk by his firm grasp of the back.

12. **St. Raising of the Body.**—The patient, standing with thighs supported against a couch or table

and hands clasped on the back of the head, bends forward as far as possible. The operator, standing behind and supporting the feet with his turned foot, places one hand on each side of the spine. The patient raises his body while the operator resists.

13. **L. Raising of the Body.**—See page 146.

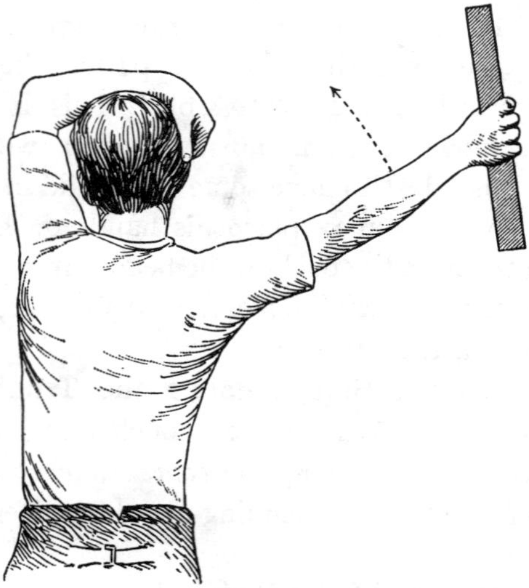

FIG. 119.

14. **St. Turning of the Body.**—The patient stands with feet closed and hands back of head. He turns from side to side with or without the operator's resistance.

15. **Raising of the Arm of the Convex Side.**—The patient is standing with the arm of the concave side flexed over the head as in Fig. 119. The arm

of the convex side is raised from the side to the head. A weight is generally used. Careful instructions in regard to respiration should be given.

16. **St. Bending of the Knees; Book on Head ("Deep Knee-Bend").** The hands are placed on the hips with fingers in front; the patient bends

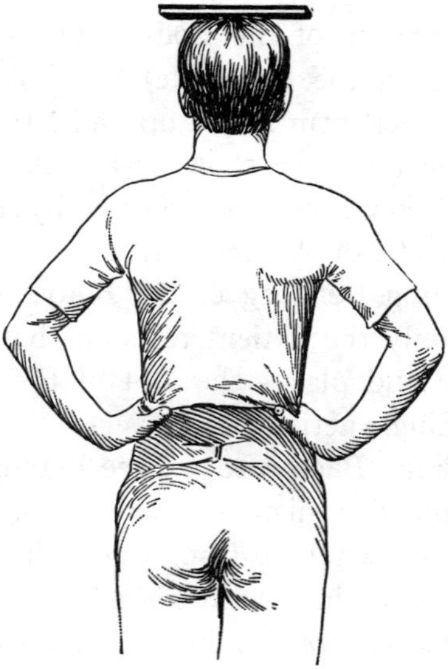

FIG. 120.

slowly downward, counting: (1) raising on the tiptoes; (2) bending down as far as possible; (3) resuming tiptoes position; (4) back to original standing position (see Fig. 120). The effort of keeping the body erect in balancing makes this a very useful exercise in the earlier stages of curvatures. The operator should watch the patient carefully to see that the proper position is maintained from start to finish.

17. **Stretch-standing Bending of the Knees.**—Similar to 16, only the patient stands with his arms stretched upward close to his ears, as shown in Fig. 54.

18. **St. Bending of the Body.**—The right (if the convexity is on the *right* side) foot forward; right hand on hip; left arm raised up and left hand down the back, between the shoulder-blades; the patient should bend slowly forward. Generally single active, but may also be duplicated active.

19. **Kneeling Bending of the Body.**—Same exercise as 18, only the patient rests on the knee of the *concave* side and places the foot of the *convex* side forward. Single active.

20. **Bending Backward; Free-standing.**—"The patient stands at a distance somewhat less than the length of his own foot from the wall. He places his hands on his hips with his elbows well thrown back. Then he *stretches* himself and bends backward. When the movement can not be continued any farther, the patient falls back until the back of his head touches the wall by which he stands. Then he slowly rises up on his toes, and while doing so draws a deep inspiration and goes slowly down again" (Kellgren).

21. **St. Bending of the Head Forward and Backward.**—The patient stands with his hands against

the wall and with his feet about twenty inches from the wall; the operator places his hand on the back of the patient's head and resists in the movement. This movement is very effective, and the author suggests that the reader have it applied to himself so as to personally feel its effect upon the different muscles of the back.

22. **St. Stretching of the Vertebral Column.**—This is a new movement, recommended by the well-known Mr. H. Kellgren, of London. The patient stands as straight as possible; the operator stands in front of him and places one hand on the patient's head, and with the other he steadies him by placing it over the sternum or abdomen; he presses firmly down with the hand on the head, while the patient is told to *stretch* upward as far as possible. Be careful to see that it does not become only a simple raising of the shoulders. We want a stretching of the whole spinal column.

23. **Susp. Bending of the Head.**—The patient is suspended a few inches from the floor. The operator, standing at his side, places one hand on the forehead, the other on the back of his head. The patient moves the head forward and backward, the operator resisting, according to the strength.

24. **Susp. Separating and Closing of Legs.**—If the patient is weak, make the movement active at first, while the operator supports the sides. Afterward make it concentric, the operator grasping around the ankles.

25. **Susp. Flexion of Legs upon the Abdomen.**—The patient is suspended and flexes his extended limbs upon the abdomen. This is a very strong movement and should be used only when the patient's strength allows.

It is very important to watch the patient in regard to his *position* for each movement. A rest should be given after every exercise, and it may be well to mention that the most complete rest is obtained when the patient lies flat on his abdomen with pillows under chest and stomach. Measure the patient's height; also curvature itself. This is best done by putting the end of the tape-measure on the vertebra corresponding to the extreme point of the convexity; carry it forward over the highest point of the convexity to the sternum or a fixed point of the sternum; then measure the concave side in the same manner and you will know from time to time how your patient improves. Always have a set rule to measure either before or after taking the movements. It becomes the operator's absolute duty to explain to the patient the tedious process of the treatment and the patient's *own* responsibility in regard to the final result. Exercise should be taken every morning and evening in the patient's own home. The results are remarkably good if proper judgment is used in the selection of movements. This treatment for curvature of the spine is very little known in America, but if given a fair trial, and the movements properly performed, many unfortunates might be saved from being crippled for life.

A few cases of Pott's disease have been treated by the author. Massage of back and chest with respiratory movements were given with good results. Of course it will be understood that there was no inflammatory process going on in the spinal column at the time of treatment. By the use of the pneumauxetor the author fully convinced himself of the increased respiratory capacity. The patients would invariably express themselves as feeling more able to hold the head and thorax erect and the increased respiratory power was always a great relief in this very trying deformity.

SPRAINS

A sprain is a sudden dislocation with a quick replacement of a joint. By the bursting of some smaller veins and lymphatics there is quite an effusion in and around the joint; the sooner that fluid is worked away mechanically the better for the patient. It seems impossible to comprehend that many surgeons still use plaster of Paris casts in the treatment of ordinary sprains, when massage properly applied will effect a cure in a short time.

In sprains it is necessary to begin with slight, careful *introductory* massage, in the form of centripetal stroking, the pain being very severe. The strength of the manipulation must not be increased until most of the swelling is gone, and the operator must be very careful to work upon every part in the neighborhood of the joint, applying, as a rule, stroking only. Then begin kneading the muscles and tendons, always ending with stroking. The treatment is greatly assisted by water applications at night. A flannel or rubber bandage must be used to keep the swelling down. Some authors recommend movements from the beginning, but I have found the best results from the *massage alone.*

In contraction of the tendo Achillis, turning and rotation of the foot, also flexion and extension, ought to be used after the fifth treatment.

The weakness of the joint after a sprain is frequently relieved by massage, the operator being careful to apply properly the bandage after each séance.

DISLOCATIONS

Inasmuch as "a sprain is a sudden dislocation with a quick replacement of a joint," a reduced dislocation is treated very much like an ordinary sprain. Precautions must however be taken to avoid a recurrence until adjoining ligaments, bands and muscles have gained sufficient strength to normally hold the articulation.

For the first few days it is therefore necessary to fix the joint with a bandage, which must be removed daily, when the joint is given a light effleurage and some passive movements to avoid stiffness.

In the course of a few days the bandage can be removed altogether, but the massage treatment must be kept up long after the pain and swelling have subsided.

The initial swelling may be considerably checked and even reduced by the application of ice bandages,

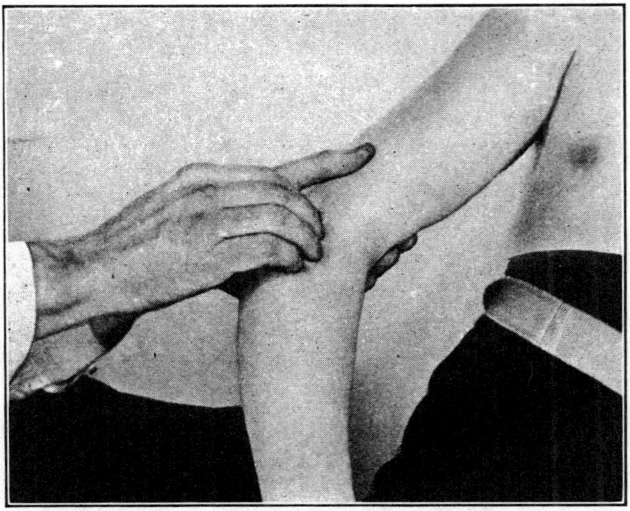

FIG. 121.—Centripetal Strokings with Tips of Fingers in Dislocated, Fractured or Sprained Elbow Joint.

and later on, hot applications, preceding each massage treatment, will add considerably to its effectiveness.

I want to take this opportunity to warn against the prevailing practice of immobilization and fixation of a reduced dislocation or a sprained joint. It is doubly wrong. First it prevents a good blood supply so much needed to repair injury, and as Dr. Mennel in his excellent work on massage says: "By absolute rest the circulation in the part is reduced to a minimum and this is all the more pernicious on account of the vaso-motor disturbance due to the injury.

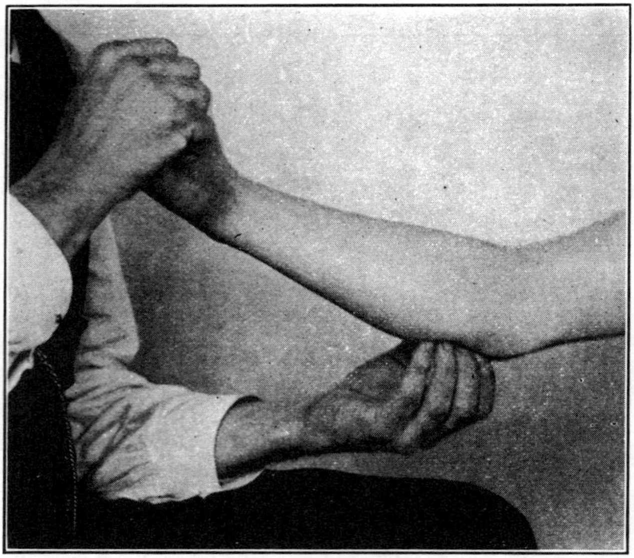

FIG. 122.—Examining the Mobility of an Injured Elbow Joint.

In all these injuries the surrounding muscles undergo a rapid wasting, due to a reflex set up in the joint, which derives its nerve supply from the same sources as do the muscles, and by immobilization there is nothing done to counteract this wasting. This points out the importance of an early massage and movement treatment of not only the joint, but of the adjoining muscles as well.—[*Editor.*]

SYNOVITIS

Massage is always indicated in cases of synovitis, so long as there is no purulent inflammation. The

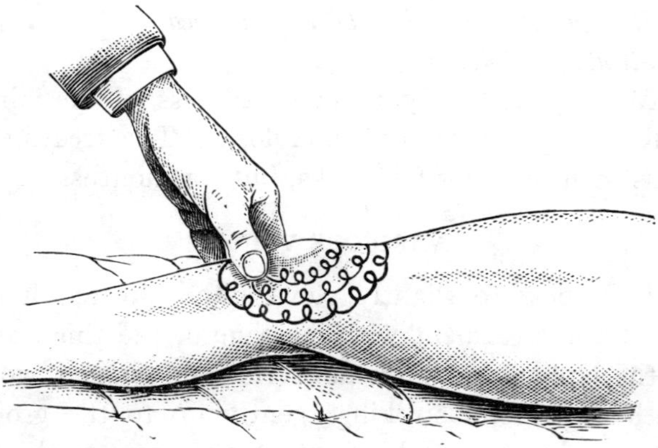

FIG. 123.—Friction with the Thumb in Cases of Synovitis of the Knee-joint.

introductory massage, in the form of centripetal stroking, is to be used with great care. When the pain is diminished some passive movements may be applied, as flexion and extension. If the joint be very sore, as is usually the case, work in its neighborhood with kneading and stroking.

In chronic inflammation of the joints it is always necessary to pay special attention to atrophied muscles above and below the joint. Friction (with strokings followed) is the most effective manipulation around joints (see Fig. 123).

In ankylosis always apply very hot water before every séance.

Evald Johnsen, a Scandinavian masseur, out of 137 cases of synovitis, cured 94 perfectly, improved 39 and treated only 4 without any result.

The patient must not be kept in bed, but must use his limbs as much as possible.

Massage not only relieves stiffness of the joint, but also prevents total ankylosis. The treatment must continue not for weeks, but for months.

VARICOSE VEINS

It is best to slightly elevate the affected limb. Start the treatment with massage of the thigh and if the saphenous vein is not seriously inflamed, work with centripetal strokings gently up to the groin. In regard to the local treatment, the operator should avoid too strong pressure directly over the veins affected, but should try to improve the circulation in the collateral veins, thereby relieving the tension in the varicose veins. Stroking is the only safe manipulation directly over the vein, and I always use an oil made of oil of sweet almonds three (3) parts and oil of eucalyptus one (1) part. This oil prevents too strong friction and, besides being antiseptic, seems to have a soothing effect on the patient.

We must remember to use the various circulatory movements of the foot and leg.

We are used to hear persons suffering with this trouble complain about their elastic stockings being so hot and uncomfortable during warm weather. I have used lately with great satisfaction the "Bender Elastic Bandage" or "Maximum" bandage of elastic stockings.

In cases of subacute phlebitis we use similar treatment as here described for varicose veins, except that we are safer in using more direct pressure over the veins.

HERNIA

Many cases of recent hernia have been successfully treated by massage. The patient is placed flat on his back without headrest, so as to relax the muscles of the abdomen. We massage the muscles in a general way at first and afterwards locally, the object being to so strengthen the muscular parts around the ring that the normal retentive power is established. I have used with great satisfaction the Iodine Vasogen 7 per cent. with this treatment.

There is no use of trying manual treatment for this trouble unless the patient can be made to fully understand that he is not to stand up without his truss on.

In a severe case a surgical operation is of course necessary for a complete cure. The patient should be instructed in the useful hernia-movements recommended by Dr. George H. Taylor, of New York.

FRACTURES

Since the ambulatory treatment of fractures has been described by Krause in Germany and by Hood and Sir William Bennett, of England, the American surgeons seem to begin to take to it more in a few selected cases.

Every simple fracture of the extremities should be treated by massage before being reduced; we can, by gentle manipulations above and around the fracture, draw the effusions away. The nearer a joint the fracture, the more important the massage becomes. The operator should of course be very careful in handling the injured member and it is necessary to have someone to assist in supporting it.

In fracture of the patella we must take special care of the quadriceps extensor femoris and we must prevent adhesions of the fragments above and below. In giving the massage around the knee we hold the fragments together with the thumb and index finger of one hand and work with the other hand.

In severe fractures with complications treated by the old method the masseur is often called upon to deal with some difficult conditions. Where there is impaired motion from faulty nerve or muscle action the operator should carefully find out which muscles are the weaker and massage them; he should also overcome contractions of the antagonists by movements or splints even, if necessary.

Strokings of the inside of the whole extremity affected are necessary to restore the circulation. Anyone interested in the treatment of fractures should read the two following books: "Massage in

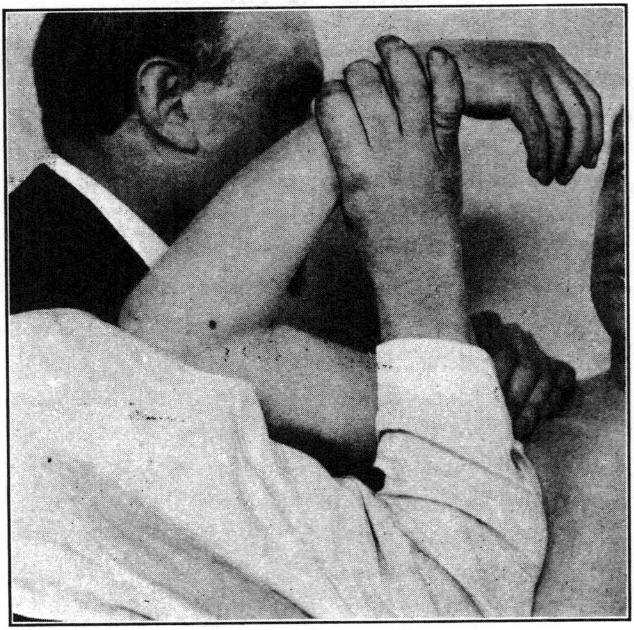

FIG. 124.—Forcing a Stiff Elbow-joint.

Recent Fractures," by Sir William Bennett, and "The Treatment of Injuries," by Dr. Wharton P. Hood.

The active movements are sometimes indicated. In Figs. 124 and 125 we have represented two different ways of forcing contracted limbs and stiff joints. The practical operator will see at a glance the great benefit obtained from the positions given.

DEFORMITIES OF THE FEET

In cases of club-foot use massage on the foot and on the leg up to the knee. A few turnings and flexions are very beneficial.

In cases of "pigeon-toes" use similar treatment as for club-foot, but with the massage extended up to the hip.

Also the following movements:

1. St. turning of the leg outward.
2. St. rotation of ext. leg (semicircle).
3. L. separating and closing of knees.
4. Feet at more than right angle, deep knee-bend, operator supporting chest and back.
5. Depression and elevation of legs, the operator turning the feet out as much as possible.
6. L. separating and closing of legs, feet turned out as much as possible.

In cases of flat foot we can, by the Gefvert splint and our massage and movements, cure the deformity in a comparatively short time, if the patient will only persevere and be willing to stand a little pain. Apply careful massage to the whole foot and leg up to the knee. The following movements are very effective:

1. Turning of the foot inward.

2. Rotation of the foot.
3. Flexion and extension of the foot.
4. Walking on tiptoe.
5. Walking on the outside border of the foot.
6. Feet closed; deep knee-bend.

Try to teach the patient to practice walking on his tiptoes five or six times daily. Massage is a valuable remedy in the complicated local nerve-troubles, so frequently caused by a condition of talipes valgus.

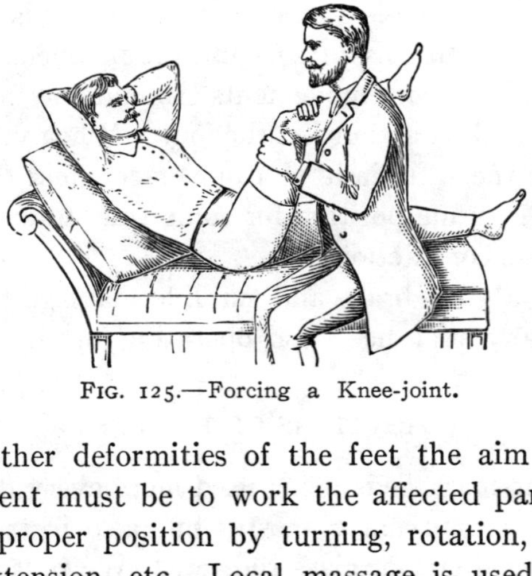

FIG. 125.—Forcing a Knee-joint.

In other deformities of the feet the aim of the treatment must be to work the affected part back to its proper position by turning, rotation, flexion and extension, etc. Local massage is used to invigorate the muscles and to relax contracted tendons.

All the deformities arising from infantile paralysis have been successfully treated by massage.

In *talipes calcaneus*, where the heel only touches the floor, we massage the posterior part of the leg to strengthen the soleus and gastrocnemius. We extend the foot by movements so as to overcome the contraction of the stronger flexor muscles. (See rules for treating paralysis on page 124.)

In *talipes equino-varus* where the toes come to the floor and the heel is drawn up and the foot *inverted* we massage the tibialis anticus, peroneus tertius and peroneus longus principally. We flex, evert and abduct the foot.

In *talipes equino-valgus* where the toes touch the floor and the heel is drawn up and the foot is *everted*, we treat the tibialis anticus and the peroneus tertius principally. Our movements should be selected so as to adduct and invert the foot. When you have reached the safe limit of a movement hold the foot in that extreme position for some time to overcome tendinous contraction.

With a good brace and suitable massage there is rarely any real need for operating on the tendo Achillis.

AFFECTIONS OF THE EYE

Ocular massage is being used more every day; we use the second finger mostly but also instruments like corneal spoon, glass rod, etc. We press either on the lid to act upon the lid itself or to act upon the ball by firmer pressure. See Fig. 25. Massage of the lid is used mostly to absorb extravasations in black-eye. The Scandinavian oculists employ ocular massage freely to hasten the complete maturation of an unripe cataract. The Russian Maklakow has invented an electric vibrator in which percussion is given by a small hammer striking the ball regularly several thousand times a minute.

Massage is used for several chronic inflammations of the eye. By local massage we increase the circulation around the eye, and act directly upon the cornea. When we desire to see more clearly we rub the eyes, instinct telling us to remove from the cornea such particles as are stagnated. Certain swellings of the eyelids have been treated with great success by massage in the clinics of Schmidt, Rimpler, Rossander and Pagenstecher.

Cases of *maculæ corneæ* (granules on the cornea) have been very successfully treated. In some cases it is wise to apply massage on the whole front part of the affected side, and also on the same side of the neck.

General massage is frequently used to strengthen the nervous system, thus giving effect upon the optic nerve.

Manual treatment must never be applied to the eye without an order from a physician.

AFFECTIONS OF THE EAR

Some authors (Politzer, Eitelberg) recommend massage for certain affections of the ear, and in my practice I have often been able to relieve severe pain, in cases of otitis, by massage only, in the form of centripetal strokings over the mastoid process and the corresponding side of the neck, as recommended by Gerst.

In a few cases local massage has been applied to the ear with good results (Meyer and Lautenbach). As in chronic congestive headaches, (see page 121), massage of the liver and the cervical and dorsal nerves is of greatest benefit in many ear-conditions. In a case of catarrhal deafness of long standing the author has clearly demonstrated that perfect hearing was restored for several hours after each treatment. Suspending bending of the head, concentric is also of great help, relieving as it does the congestion of the many vessels of the neck. Bending rotation and turning of the head are also useful movements.

GENERAL REMARKS

I. It is rather difficult to fix the time for a massage treatment. Dr. Mezger works only a few minutes (five to twelve minutes), but I am satisfied that he accomplishes more in that time than many do in half an hour. As a rule, use shorter time for a local than for a constitutional affection.

In the rest-cure some eminent physicians begin with fifteen to twenty minutes, gradually increasing the time to an hour or even longer.

II. The weakest person may be treated by massage, since it is a remedy so easily adapted to circumstances and so perfectly controlled.

III. The patient ought not feel any severe pain or disagreeable fatigue after the treatment. Should such be the effect; stop the treatment for a few days, and on resuming it regulate the pressure carefully.

IV. After each treatment the patient should rest for at least half an hour in a comfortable position.

V. The patient should be urged to refrain from excessive eating and drinking, and the treatment should not be applied within two hours after meals.

VI. The operator must breathe freely while giving the treatment, and must be in a proper position, neither too close to the patient nor too far off.

VII. The temperature of the room should be 70°–75° F.; the operator should always be careful to cover up the part massaged and avoid having any draft from windows or doors.

VIII. The operator should possess good health and muscular strength. He should be cheerful and of refined habits, and should have a fair education, with a perfect knowledge of the principal facts in anatomy and physiology.

IX. *Massage treatment is an art which can not be self-acquired, but must be taught by an experienced instructor.*

X. The manual treatment of disease ought to be regulated by the medical profession; hence the physician's order should be properly carried out, even though the operator be of a different opinion.

XI. A student of massage should have the treatment applied to his own body, by that ascertaining the proper pressure to be used upon the various tissues.

THE MASSAGE TREATMENT IN AMERICA

There is no medical agency that has been so much abused as massage. When I came to America I was anxious to find out how the manual treatment of disease was carried on here. I soon learned that there were no laws requiring registration, but that I could find the masseurs through the physicians and the daily papers. I visited several of these, and submitted myself to treatment by some. I discovered there was no science whatever in their treatment; some seemed to entirely ignore the fact that nature had provided me with sensitive nerves. Most of these operators used no oil, and consequently the hair bulbs of the limbs operated on by them became inflamed. I do not know where they had acquired their knowledge of massage, or, as they termed it, "the rubbing." One of them was sure that he had an inherited power of magnetism, etc., because his father had been "a prominent rubber" in Germany. Another, I understood, had been working in a hospital, and while the buildings were undergoing repair he was offered a position in the basement,—whether to wash dishes or not, I could not find out,—but he declined, and left the place to become "a rubber," and is rubbing still.

Not only is the massage treatment practised by such persons whose muscular power should be exerted on something less sensitive than the diseased and weakened human body, but it has also been used as a disguise for vicious purposes.

It is reported that the police in Chicago have raided a number of "massage shops," and one of the leading daily papers of Philadelphia asserted that a raid had been made upon similar houses in this city, where the massage treatment was used as a cloak for vice.

So long as there is an abundant supply of both masseurs and masseuses, there is no necessity that a woman should be treated by a man, or a man by a woman. There are, of course, exceptions, as, for instance, that of a trained *scientific* masseur or of a trained female nurse who is attending a patient in his family.

I see no reason why such a powerful, remedial agency as massage should not be fully controlled by the medical profession, as it is in Europe.

It seems to me that the physician who recommends an incompetent person to attend his patients does wrong, and we have frequently heard sad experiences from patients whose social standing ought to have protected them from being imposed upon by incompetent, uneducated persons.

Some time ago there was a masseur in this city who was given a case of sprain at the ankle-joint. The surgeon performed a very slight flexion of the foot, so as to ascertain the amount of contraction in the tissues around the joint. At one of the first séances this masseur thought he would repeat the flexion and a fracture was the result.

Such things are unpleasant to bring before the public, but it is quite proper they should be noticed in a text-book on massage, when there is danger that one of the most natural and powerful medical agencies will be neglected because it has not been duly protected, but practised by persons who would be more appropriately employed at the wash-tub or in the kitchen.

Let me now say a few words about educated practitioners of the manual treatment. Some of them, and especially females, have been accused of thinking too much of themselves, of being too independent. Masseurs and masseuses should remember that they are only using one special remedy that nature has taught man to employ to arrest disease. Persons who are properly trained will not attempt to enter into competition with medical doctors, but confine themselves to the scientific treatment that we have endeavored to analyze in this little text-book.

Were it not for abuses that have prevailed, the manual treatment of disease would no doubt be more universally adopted and recommended by the medical profession and the general public.

From this short sketch we conclude:

1. That the massage and movement treatments

should be applied only by educated and properly trained persons, with due regard to the physician's directions.

2. That the operator (if not a medical doctor) should be of the same sex as the patient, with only the two exceptions before mentioned.

3. That there should be a place where skilful and trained operators could have an opportunity for passing an examination and for registering, thus protecting not only themselves and the profession, but *the general public* as well.

BIBLIOGRAPHY

For the convenience of those who desire to study especially certain branches of mechanotherapeutics I herewith give a list of some of the English literature on the subject.

Abrams, Albert.—"The Blues." "Spondylo-Therapy."

Althaus, J.—"The Risks of Massage," "British Medical Journal," London, 1883. I. 1223.

Bacot, J.—"Observations on the Use and Abuse of Friction," etc. London, 1888.

Baynes, Donald.—"Auxiliary Methods of Cure: Massage," etc. London, 1888.

Bennett, Sir William.—"Massage in Recent Fractures." London, 1903.

Block, S.—"Massage." New York, 1885.

Bloom, Homer C.—"A Clinical Study in Pelvic Massage." "Journal Am. Med. Asso.," April 30, 1898.

Blundell, J. W. F.—"Cases of Neuralgia, Rheumatism, etc., Successfully Treated by Swedish Movements." London, 1856.

Bullock.—"Massage in the Treatment of Disease." "Louisville Medical News," 1885. XX, 401–403.

Butler, J.—"Electro-Massage." Philadelphia, 1881.

Comstock, A.—"Massage Therapy." "Therapeutic Gazette," Detroit, 1888. IV, 602–605.

Dowse, Thomas Stretch.—"The Modern Treatment of Disease by Massage." (Lectures.) London, 1887.

"The Treatment of Disease by Physical Methods." New York, 1899.

Eccles, A. S.—"The Practice of Massage." New York, 1898.
"Massage in Dyspepsia and in Sleeplessness." "British Medical Journal," London, 1887. II, 502–504.

Ellison, M. A.—"A Manual for Students of Massage." London, 1898.

Franks, K.—"Reports on Massage." "Dublin Journal of Medical Science," 1889. LXXXVIII, 241–250.

Garry, T. G.—"Massage as a Curative Agent." "Lancet," London, 1888. I, 921.

Grafstrom, Axel.—"A Text-book of Mechano-Therapy." Philadelphia, 1899.

Graham, Douglass.—"Massage." "Medical and Surgical Reporter," Philadelphia, 1874. XXXI, 181–188.
"Massage in Amenorrhea and Dysmenorrhea," "Boston Medical and Surgical Journal," 1876. XCIV, 146–150.
"The History of Massage." "Medical Record," New York, 1879. XVI, 147–171.
"A Practical Treatise on Massage." New York, 1884.

Grant, D.—"On Massage." "Edinburgh Medical Journal," 1887–'88. XXXIII, 35–39, 119–124.

Granville, I. M.—"Nerve Vibration as a Therapeutic Agent." "Lancet," London, 1882. I, 949–951.

Hood, Wharton P.—"Treatment of Injuries." London, 1903.

Jackson, A. Reeves.—"Uterine Massage as a Means of Treating Certain Forms of the Enlargement of the Womb." "Boston Medical and Surgical Journal," 1880. CIII, 388–391.

Jones, H. M.—"The Use and Abuse of Massage in Gynecological Practice." "British Gynecological Journal," London, 1889–'90. V, 89–105.

Keen, W. W.—"Passive Exercise on the Production of Albuminuria." "Medical and Surgical Reporter," Philadelphia, 1885. LIII, 333.

Kellgren, Arvid.—"Technic of Manual Treatment." Edinburgh, 1890.

Kellogg, J. H.—"The Art of Massage." Battle Creek, Michigan, 1895.

Kleen, Emil.—"Handbook of Massage." Philadelphia, 1892.

Little, J. F.—"Medical Rubbing." "British Medical Journal," London, 1882. II, 351.

Martin, F. H.—"Massage: its Application." "Chicago Medical Journal and Examiner," 1883. XLVII, 26–34.

Mennell, James B.—"Massage, Its Principles and Practice." Philadelphia and London, 1917.

Mills, Charles K.—"Proper and Improper Methods of Performing Massage." "Polyclinic," Philadelphia, 1886–'87. IX, 111–116.

Murrell, W.—"Massage as a Mode of Treatment." Philadelphia, 1890.

Muller, George.—"Spinal Curvature," etc. London, 1904.

Nissen, H.—"Manual for Instruction in Giving Massage and Swedish Movements." Philadelphia, 1889.

Ostrom, Kurre W.—"Massage in the Treatment of Sprains." "Medical and Surgical Reporter," Philadelphia, January 4, 1890.

Palmer, Marg. D.—"Lessons on Massage," London, 1901.

Posse, Baron Nils.—"The Therapeutic Applications of Medical Gymnastics." "Boston Medical and Surgical Journal," 1889. CXX, 459–462.

"School-Gymnastics," Boston, 1891.

Post, Sarah E.—"Massage Primer." New York, 1891.

Reibmayer, Albert.—(Translated by Dr. B. Lee.)—"Tracts on Massage." I, II, III. Philadelphia, 1885.

Ryley, I. B.—"Remarkable Effects of Massage on Gastric Assimilation and Nervous Debility." "Lancet," London, 1883. I, 946.

Smith, A. J.—"On the Treatment of Prolapse of the Uterus by Massage and Pelvic Gymnastics." "Medical Press and Circular," London, 1888. N. S., XLVII, 560–562.

Smith, A. J.—"A Brief Outline of Dr. Zander's Institution in Stockholm." "Lancet," London, 1881. I, 860–862.

Snell, S.—"On Massage in Certain Eye Affections." "Ophthalmological Review," London, 1888. VII, 134–139.

Soderberg, John.—"Swedish Manual Treatment." London, 1898.

Sturge, W. K.—"Klemm on Muscle Beating." "London Medical Recorder," 1878. VI, 290.

Taylor, C. F.—"The Movement Cure, with Cases." New York, 1888.

Tibbits, Herbert.—"Massage and its Application." London, 1887.

White, W. A.—"On Massage and the Weir Mitchell Treatment." "Guy's Hospital Report," London, 1888. 3d S., XXX, 267–286.

Wide, Anders.—"Handbook of Medical Gymnastics." New York, 1899.

Williams, Edward.—"The Revived. Ancient Art of Massage," etc. London, 1888.

Von Noorden, Carl.—"Obesity." New York, 1903.
"The Technique of Reduction Cures," New York, 1904.

Zeigenspeck, Rob.—"Massage Treatment in Diseases of Women." Translated by Westerschulte. Chicago, 1898.

INDEX